TALES OF HORSEMANSHIP

"The Carson James method is whatever works for the horse. My goal is to be able to break it down for people into very small pieces that are really simple and easy to understand just like I try to do when I'm helping my horses learn."

- Carson James

TALES OF HORSEMANSHIP
AN INSIDE LOOK AT THE SECRETS OF SUCCESSFUL HORSE TRAINING REVEALED THROUGH SHORT STORIES

CARSON JAMES

CarsonJames.com LLC

TALES OF HORSEMANSHIP
AN INSIDE LOOK AT THE SECRETS OF SUCCESSFUL HORSE TRAINING REVEALED THROUGH SHORT STORIES

Published by:
CarsonJames.com LLC

ISBN 978-0-9997998-0-2 paperback
ISBN 978-0-9997998-1-9 eBook

Edited by:
Julie Rhodenizer
Jared Rhodenizer

Cover Design by:
Jared Rhodenizer

Cover Photography:
Andi Harmon

Interior Design by:
Jared Rhodenizer

Illustrations by:
Julijana Mijailovic

DEDICATION

To my dad, who taught me how to treat people the right way and how to always remain humble in every situation.

To my mom, who is my biggest fan and is always there for me whenever I need her.

To my wife, Brooke, who has always supported all my endeavors. You are a true companion, and I love being with you.

And to my brother, Jared, who helped me and this business become what it is today. If it weren't for you, no one would have ever known about me.

TABLE OF CONTENTS

INTRODUCTION

The stories in this book will change the way you approach your horse training. The horse you desire to have is actually right under the surface. You just have to know how to unlock his potential. This is not a how-to book about solving horse problems. But, once you grasp these clearly explained principles, you will be able to solve any horse problem on your own, and even prevent future problems. This book will explain how to have a light, consistent, respectful and willing partner. You may be thinking, 'I've heard all this before', but this book goes much deeper than simply giving you specific formulas to try. It goes inside the mind of the horse, and the horseman, to expose what is happening under the surface. It's not for someone who wants a magic bullet quick fix, and it's not for someone who believes they already know everything there is to know about horses. Tales of Horsemanship will be an invaluable resource for anyone who has a desire to improve their horsemanship, understand their horse, be a confident leader, and master communicator. It reveals the effective and practical secrets of successful horse training.

You may have owned horses your whole life and even be a better-than-average rider. But no matter how much success you've had training horses, there's always room for improvement. The ability to read a horse and then communicate in a way they can understand is an ongoing process. The vast wisdom and knowledge contained in this book has been tried and tested on thousands of horses.

Horsemanship is not learned from following steps 1, 2, and 3 or a predetermined method. It's all about understanding how the horse thinks and what makes him do what he does. The horse is never wrong. He only does what he believes is the best and easiest thing for him to do. The various 'problems' we see in the horse are only what's being revealed on surface, but there's an underlying reason for his behavior that we need to discover. Once we truly understand what's happening inside the horse and can communicate on his level, all the problems will melt away.

We can't communicate properly until we learn how to read the horse and identify when he's trying, when he's not trying, when to add pressure, and when to reward. Once you get that down, you become the leader your horse willing follows and wants to be with. You feel of him, you feel, for him, and then you both feel together. This is where harmony and unity merge and it all comes together. No matter how capable or incapable you believe you are right now, this book will help you be better. Horsemanship is an acquired skill that anyone can learn. Some people have a natural gift of being able to sing. They are born with it. But horsemanship is not a gift. It can be taught, learned, and applied effectively with correct knowledge and understanding. And anyone can do it. Even if you've tried different programs, or read many other books and articles, give me the benefit of the doubt, and let me share some principles that you may have not heard or thought about before.

In this book, you'll discover...

- How to get inside the mind of your horse
- How to speak the horse's language
- How to become a confident leader
- How to have the proper timing and approach
- How to ensure your horse's respect
- How to become the owner your horse wants you to be

Trying to solve individual horse problems is like pruning a thorn bush. You clip off one thorn after another in an attempt to cause the thorn bush to no longer produce thorns. But, the root of the thorn is unchanged, so it will continue to produce more thorns. However, if you can change the root, that will change what is produced. If you could dig up that root and replace it with the root of a pear tree, the same ground would then produce pears instead of thorns. Horsemanship changes the root. Once you apply horsemanship, you'll find that your problems are no longer there and the fruit that is produced from your horse is exactly what you've always wanted. You no longer have the horse that has be to in front on the trail. You no longer have the horse that would rather be with his buddy instead of you. You no longer have the horse that is always wanting to go faster than you are. You longer have the horse that doesn't pay attention. You no longer have a horse doesn't 'respect' you.

You now have a horse that can...

- See you as a confident leader
- Keep his focus and attention on you
- Quickly and willingly respond
- Try harder every day to please you

But before we get started, it's critical to understand what true horsemanship really is. There's a lot of fluff, gimmicks, and half-truths out there that have veered away from what great horseman of the past knew and taught. This book goes back to the authentic principles of Real. Simple. Horsemanship.

CHAPTER 1
WHAT IS HORSEMANSHIP?

You can look online right now and find about 10,000 programs for training horses, and all 10,000 of those programs would probably work if you knew how to apply them in a way where the horse could understand. The problem with a lot of the training out there in the interwebs is that they give you a definitive response system. For example, if your horse is buddy sour, then here's step 1, 2, and 3 on how to fix him. But my question is, "What if my horse doesn't do that? What if my horse does this, that, or something completely unexpected? Then what?" See, that's the problem with following a program that teaches you step 1, 2, and 3. You're only learning what to do, but not how or why you're doing it. That's why someone, for example, could watch a program on TV, go outside and copy the exact steps on their horse, and it might not work. If your timing was off, and you had the wrong approach, it wouldn't matter what you did; it would eventually fall apart.

A big part of horsemanship is learning the how and the why. It would be nice if we could just look up a solution in the horse dictionary and instantly know exactly what to do. Unfortunately horses don't work that way. They're not like computers that have a definitive and consistent response each and every time.

And look, I get it. You're not trying to win the horse trainer of the year award (if that's even real). You're just trying to enjoy time spent with your horse, build your relationship stronger, and have confidence in knowing the work you're putting in isn't a waste of time. But wouldn't it be nice if you could assess the horse, know exactly what needed to be done to help him understand, and then he began to do (or not do) what you were asking? What if you started working with your horse using one program or "method", and if that didn't work, you immediately knew what to do to fill in the gaps? The second your horse stopped understanding, you had another approach to get him back on track.

How? Because you acquired something much, much deeper than following a 10 step training program. You learned horsemanship. If you have good horsemanship, you can mix and match all kinds of different training programs, techniques, and methods that make the most sense to the horse.

I like to compare horsemanship to Granny's cooking. I know that may sound a little weird, but just stick with me here. Granny always makes the most amazing apple pie. My mom would ask Granny for the

recipe so she could make it too. Granny would always say, "Well you put a pinch of this, a dab of that, stir it a little, slice up some apples, etc." There was no specific recipe that Granny followed. She just knew what to do because she knew how to cook. She was so good that she could dip her spoon into a pot of stew, taste it, and know exactly what it needed and how much of it. Mom would try to make the apple pie like Granny's, but it never tasted as good as Granny's (sorry Mom).

Once you learn horsemanship, you're like Granny. You begin filling in where it's needed and you just know what to do because you understand horses. You're not tied down to following the recipe because you don't need a recipe. You're an amazing cook! And even if you did follow a recipe, and it didn't turn out well, you'd know what was needed to fix it.

And here's the good news about horsemanship. Anyone can learn it. It's not something that you're born with. It's an acquired skill (just like cooking). When I was a kid, I used to be into airplanes, and I wanted to be a pilot when I grew up. I didn't know much of anything about horses. But since horsemanship is an acquired skill, I was able to learn it and put it to work. Throughout this book you're going to be reading stories of how horsemanship was used in many different scenarios to accomplish what was needed to help the horse understand. And it may even start to sound repetitive because you're going to realize that horsemanship is basically doing the exact same thing in many different ways. But before we get into the stories, I think it's critical that we define what horsemanship is. I define it as the ability to read the horse, come to his level, and reply with the appropriate timing and approach to help him understand.

What Is Timing?

Timing is how horses are trained. It's the key to everything. Timing goes hand-in-hand with pressure and release. You have to be particular and make sure you get the timing right when you add or release pressure. A second too soon or too late can mean the difference in your horse "getting it" or being confused.

I define pressure as making something uncomfortable to the

CONFUSED HORSE

horse Note that I said uncomfortable, not painful. To make something uncomfortable, you get in the horse's way. You make it difficult for them when they don't do what you are asking them to do. Release is the exact opposite. When the horse does want you want, you get out of their way, and make it really easy for them. Whenever you add pressure to the horse (by getting in his way), hold that pressure until the horse finds his way out of it by making a positive change, and don't give up. Once he makes a positive change, your job is to provide an instant, immediate

UNDERSTANDING HORSE

release of pressure and get out of their way.

In some cases, if the horse isn't making the change, you may need to add more pressure, use less pressure, or maintain the pressure you have and wait longer until you see the change. It just depends. Other times you may need to hold steady pressure and wait. For example, a colt that has never been ridden is not going to lope a perfect circle no matter how hard you pull.

Over time, as the horse begins to understand, less and less pressure will be necessary to get him to respond quicker and more accurately to what you're asking him to do. This is what creates a horse that is "light".

However, with that said, you usually must be "heavy" with your horse before he can learn to become light.

Offer The "Good Deal" First

In some circles of the horse world, there is a prevailing thought that if you ever use more than featherlight pressure, you're not a good horser (my word). People have adopted the "natural" philosophy and assumed that to create a light horse, you must handle them lightly all the time, and if you ever use more than two ounces of pressure, you're going to make your horse heavy. So, well-intentioned riders treat their horse with kid gloves all the time, and the horse ends up getting the bad end of the deal because communication is hindered, and the horse is never enabled to reach his full potential.

The critical key is the timing of when you're light and when you're heavy. The goal is to be light as possible, but as firm as necessary. Always offer the horse "the good deal" first.

To do this, you'll always start out with very light pressure, and then if nothing happens, turn up the heat and start adding more pressure until you see a small change. This gives the horse a reason to respond to the lighter pressure and teaches him that, if he'll respond to that lighter pressure first, the heavier, more uncomfortable pressure won't come.

But if the horse doesn't respond to that lighter pressure, and you don't follow up with heavier pressure, you're going to have an unresponsive horse. You just have to apply it in a way that is fair to the horse and within his level of understanding. I see so many people who almost got their horse to make that positive change, but they gave up too early. Don't give up. Hang in there until you get a change. There will be many examples of this throughout this book.

Make It The Horse's Idea

When you get good at timing, you'll be able to apply the pressure so the horse thinks the pressure is self-inflicted. If the horse thinks he's the one causing the pressure, it will help prevent him from getting sour, having a bad attitude, or being resistant. Plus, it will be much more effective.

Imagine you had a horse that would try to bite you when you tightened the cinch on the saddle. One way to work on this would be to let the horse run into pressure every time he started to reach his head back towards you. You could hold an object in your hand and as soon as you noticed the horse starting to reach his head around, raise that object up between you and the horse's head. When the horse reaches around, he's going to smack right into it. Did you hit the horse or did the horse run into the object? The horse ran into the object.

Eventually the horse is going to stop reaching around because every time he does it, he runs into pressure. And he also believes that this pressure is self inflicted. In his brain he'll start to figure out that every time he reaches around, it's uncomfortable. Now again, this is why timing is so critical. If you were late putting the object up, you'd be hitting him. He'd already have nipped at you or bitten you and anything you did past that point would be too late. The pressure wouldn't be self inflicted. Usually when I explain this concept to the horse owner, they'll respond by saying, "I already do that." But then when I do what they thought they were doing, there is a different outcome. It's not what you do, it's how you do it. If they were actually doing what they thought they were doing, they wouldn't be having the problem.

Horses Don't Do Wrong Or Right

Something you also need to keep in mind with horses is that they never do anything right or wrong. I want to say that again so you really get it. Horses don't do anything right or wrong. Horses do what you make feel good to them. So if you make one action feel better than the other, they will always follow the path of least resistance. How do you make one action feel better than the other? You pave that path by showing them which is easier than the other by using pressure and release. Make one path easy and make everything else more difficult.

Think about deer. They have game trails that they walk on through the woods. Why? Because walking on the trail is easier than walking off the trail. Animals (and humans, too) will always look for the path of least resistance, and once they find it, they will take it. Just look at all the products that have been invented to make our lives easier. To be a master horseman is to become a master of paving the path of least resistance. Once we get this down, the horse will almost train himself.

Imagine a horse that rears up when asked to back up. Is it not easier to back up than to rear and flip over backwards? Well, of course it is. But you have to be able to see that, in this horse's mind, he is convinced that the best thing to do is rear. And this is always because the human has been unknowingly training him to rear. And then, finally, the horse did exactly what he was trained to do. If he knew of something better to do, he would do that instead.

So many times we see a horse that is trying his hardest to figure the human out, but with the approach the human has, he simply cannot do it. And then the horse gets blamed for being disrespectful, lazy, inattentive, etc. However, the horse has no other choice but to do these things. He's doing the best thing he knows to do for the situation. Our job is to pave a different, easier path. It's never the horse that makes the adjustment. It's always the human.

Any sane person wouldn't get in an airplane and just try to take off and fly without the basic knowledge of how to operate it. But for some reason, many people are willing to do this with a horse and then wonder why they have trouble. They read an article online, listen to a friend, or watch a video and then go outside and attempt to train their horse to do something. Imagine if you did this with an airplane. Would you watch a video about how to operate a plane and then jump in one and try to take off? Of course you wouldn't (hopefully). And we shouldn't do this with our horses either. I have a pilot's license, and trust me when I tell you, horses are much more complicated than airplanes. People often try to blame the horse for the issues they're having, but it's not the horse's fault. If you're not operating the horse correctly, it's your fault. If you wrecked an airplane, without the knowledge of how to operate it, it wouldn't be the airplane's fault.

The Approach

The approach you use is also critical. First you need to recognize that when you approach a horse and attempt to teach him something new, it's going to be a big deal to the horse. Don't go into training a horse thinking that the horse is just supposed to understand what you're wanting. Many people assume that a horse should know certain things, but this isn't true at all. Always start with the mindset that the horse is completely clueless as to what's happening. This way of thinking

will help keep you in check and aid in preventing you from getting too frustrated.

However, if you've been working with your horse, and he's shown you that he does understand, then you can start expecting more out of him.

People mess up because they try to work with the horse at the level they think he's at, or the level they think he SHOULD be at, instead of working with the horse at the level he's actually at. Learn to identify and accept where your horse is at, and then work with him to bring him up to the level you want him at.

Another approach that you will see me using throughout this entire book is breaking things down into steps. Horses can't see the big picture like we can, and they can only focus on doing one thing at a time. They also don't know the end goal. But once you figure out a way to break the training exercise apart into multiple pieces, and just work on one piece at a time, you'll have more success.

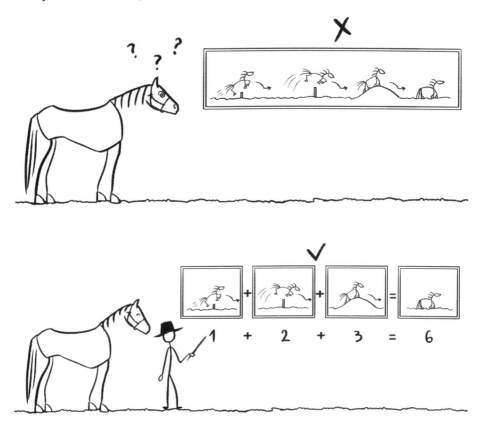

The Horse's Personality

Now you may be thinking, 'what about personalities'? Well, yes, each horse has a different personality, but that personality doesn't override their overall horse nature. Once you learn good horsemanship, you'll be able to adjust and help the horse to understand, no matter what his personality is.

When asked about a horse's personality, I often refer to Johnny. He was always a really goofy kid. He loved to entertain and loved to make people laugh. Then he decided to go into the military. The drill sergeant didn't put up with Johnny's goofiness while on the clock. When working, Johnny had to do everything like he was told. And he did because he understood that the drill sergeant was in charge. Does this mean Johnny lost his personality? No. When Johnny left boot camp and came back home, he was still the fun loving guy that everyone loved, but he learned to have respect for his drill sergeant and do what was asked of him. It's the same with your horse.

You should expect your horse to pay attention and treat you as the leader when you're working with them. Then when they're "off the clock" and out in the pasture, they can go back to whatever personality they want.

With that said, I am a firm believer that every interaction you have with your horse is an opportunity to work on something, no matter how insignificant you think it may be.

Do Everything With Confidence

Horses thrive on having a confident leader to follow. And if they don't see you as a confident leader, they won't follow or trust you. Always act like nothing is a big deal, even though it may be a big deal in the horse's mind. Don't get in a hurry and rush things. Remain cool and confident at all times. Your body language should represent someone who has done this a million times, even if it's your first time. Horses can sense fear and doubt, and if they pick up on it, you're done.

Imagine a horse that's standing at the edge of a creek and afraid to cross it. Why is it that (usually) when another horse walks up beside it and then crosses the creek first, the scared horse will then follow the other horse? Because he trusts that horse as a leader. He trusts that the leading horse won't let any harm come to him. Your horse should see you like that second horse. Your horse should have full confidence that you are a worthy leader to follow and you have their best interest at heart. And even though they may be scared or unsure about something, they will allow their self preservation instinct to step aside in order to do what you are asking.

Horses can sense if you know what you're doing or if you don't. They just know. How do you know if you're doing something correct? You learn. Reading this book, for example, will provide you with a vast amount of knowledge, which will give your confidence a huge boost. With that said, you'll never be perfect and neither will I. But we can always get better.

A Story Of Confidence

Before I stop talking about confidence, I want to share a short story with you. I live in Florida, but I was up in Washington visiting my friend

Kevin. I'd never seen Seattle before, so I asked Kevin to ride with me downtown to see the sights. I wasn't so sure about it because I knew there were a lot of different roads, and it would be easy to get lost. Kevin said, "Oh, it's okay Carson. I know that town like the back of my hand.

I'll ride shotgun and be your guide." I was still a little nervous, but he seemed so confident that I became confident too. Away we went, right up the interstate. I was very excited to see the space needle.

We were only ten minutes from downtown and all of the sudden Kevin said, "Oh no!". When I asked what was wrong he said, "We missed our last two exits." At this point I was beginning to lose some of the confidence I had in Kevin's knowledge of the area. But he reassured me that it was ok, and we could just take the next exit. "Okay Carson, you're clear to get in the right hand lane to take this exit," Kevin said. As I started to merge, he frantically yelled, "Not yet! Look out!" We were almost clobbered by a passing semi truck in the right hand lane. And then Kevin said, "Now, the speed limit is 60 through here," but as I'm speeding up to 60, I see a sign that says the speed limit is 45. Kevin raised his voice and said, "No, no, no slow down! I just remembered it's actually 45 through here, and there's a cop sitting there! Sorry Carson that was my bad. And by the way we missed our exit again."

This went on for the rest of the trip and, by this point, I was tense at the wheel and the confidence I had earlier had dwindled down to zero. I had no choice but to begin ignoring Kevin. I just had to shut him out and rely on my instincts to get through the situation the best way I knew how. It turns out that Kevin didn't know the area as good as he thought he did.

So here's the point of this story. Kevin had convinced me that we could go see the sights, and it would be okay. He would be the leader. But once we started, there was nothing Kevin could do to trick me into believing that he knew what he was doing. It quickly became obvious that he didn't. The lack of leadership and communication is what took my confidence away which forced me to ignore him and become spooky. I had no other choice. Some might even say I was being disrespectful because I was ignoring him. But he gave me no other option. I was pretty barn sour after that. I didn't want to leave and go anywhere with Kevin. I never wanted to ride with Kevin again.

Now let's say it's the same scenario, but this time Kevin really does know the area. He communicates very well, and all his info is correct. It's like he is my own personal GPS. He's always calmly letting me know ahead of time where to turn and we never make a wrong move. Naturally, this time around I would be calm and stay very relaxed. I would feel like I owned that town and look forward to the next trip we had planned. I would not get the least bit nervous because I knew he had my back. This same calm and confident mental state is what we want for our horses.

Little Things Turn Into Big Things

Many people notice various small, insignificant nuisances in their horse

-- or at least the person assumes they are insignificant. For example, the horse that stands there and tosses his head. Someone may look at that and think it's just something annoying their horse does, and it's not really a big deal. But everything, and I mean everything, with horses is connected. A horse that tosses his head could (and probably does) have several other issues. These "gaps" all add up to cause bigger problems on down the road. But it is vitally important for a good horser (my word) to be particular and not overlook these 'small' things.

99% of the time when there is a "problem", where the problem is showing up is not actually where the problem is at all. That's just where you're seeing it surface. It's actually a lot deeper rooted somewhere else. But if we can clean up all these bad little spots, everything will all come together to make a nice, solid horse.

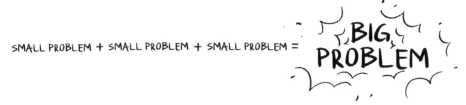

SMALL PROBLEM + SMALL PROBLEM + SMALL PROBLEM = BIG PROBLEM

An example would be a horse that had never offered to buck in six years of riding, but then, out of nowhere (in the rider's estimation), the horse just blows up. However, this major bucking issue really didn't come out of nowhere. The rider may have let a lot of smaller (or maybe unnoticed) things go on for a long time, and then one day, it all came out in the form of bucking.

So the bottom line is this. Instead of focusing on the big things, focus on the small things, and get them worked out. Be particular and don't overlook them.

The Carson James Method

In conclusion, if you go into horsing thinking you're going to follow a formula, but you don't know the WHY, and you don't have the right approach and timing, you're setting yourself up for failure. But if you understand horsemanship, you could use any method and get it to work. Heck, you could even just make up your own "method". People ask me all the time, "What's the Carson James method?" And I wind up telling everyone that there's actually not a Carson James method. My method is what works for the horse, and what helps the horse understand. I am a lifelong student of the horse, and I will always be willing to learn anything the horse wants to teach me.

There is knowledge everywhere that can help you with your horsemanship. It's all over the internet, in videos, books, audio, etc. The key is to take that knowledge, look at it under a microscope and examine WHY it worked. Once you get that, along with proper timing, you've got everything. My goal for this book is to break this knowledge down into very small pieces that are really easy and simple to understand. It's the same way I train my horses. I tear off the layers of difficulty into smaller steps which enables the horse to better understand and progress. I hope you not only enjoy, but also gain some useful knowledge, from my Tales of Horsemanship.

CHAPTER 2
CLIPPERZILLA

There was a neighbor who lived down the road from me. She knew that I trained horses, so she called to see if I could help her with a horse that was terrified of clippers. Every time she would try to trim a bridle path in the horse's mane, the horse would freak out and run backwards. One time he even ran through the fence and made a huge mess. She bet me $100 that I couldn't trim the horse's bridle path in less than an hour. I'm not much of a betting man, but I smiled politely and told her I'd take that bet. We agreed to meet up at the local arena in town.

She arrived, got this horse out of the trailer, put a halter on him, and handed him to me. Then she put the clippers in my hands and walked over to the bleachers to watch the show.

We already knew that the horse was terrified of these clippers, so the absolute wrong approach would be to start trying to trim on him. So what do we do? Well, let's zoom out and look at the bigger picture. What this horse actually needed was a boost of confidence. He was scared to death of these clippers, and was convinced they were going to hurt him bad. So we just needed to show him that's not true.

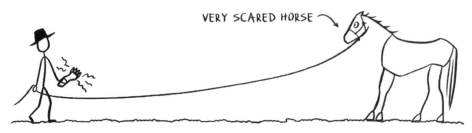

VERY SCARED HORSE

To do this, I began by standing out at the end of the lead line and turning on the clippers. As expected, the horse darted backwards away from me. But I didn't turn the clippers off. I just followed him as he backed up, and I kept the clippers on until I noticed a change. What was the change? The horse stopped walking backwards. See, if I would have turned the clippers off as he was backing up, what is that teaching him? It's teaching him that the way to get rid of the clippers is to keep backing up. And since that is the complete opposite of what we wanted, I didn't give him a reward (the clippers turning off) until he made a positive change.

It's important to note here that the reward was given for doing something very small in the big scheme of things. I was trying to get the horse to let me trim his bridle path, but I'm first rewarding him for not walking backwards. That is what breaking it down into small steps is all about. You reward the small, positive changes.

I turned on the clippers again, but this time I started about halfway down the lead line instead of at the end. This time the horse

didn't walk backwards. He just stood there all bug eyed. You could tell from his facial expression, the snorts, and the flaring nostrils that he was still terrified. But he wasn't running backwards trying to drag me across the arena, which is an improvement from when we first started. I held the clippers steady out in front of my face, and about 5 seconds later, the horse actually got a little curious and slightly tilted his nose forward

CURIOUS HORSE

to take a little inspection smell. I immediately shut the clippers off and lowered them. Why? It was another positive change. Instead of being completely terrified, the horse actually became brave enough to inspect the clippers. So I rewarded that "try".

You may be wondering, 'Well what would you do if the horse started backing up again like the first time?' I would do exactly what I did before until he didn't do it anymore. I would start at the end of the lead and follow him with the clippers until he stopped moving his feet or made some other positive change.

Anyone who is going to work with horses needs to be prepared that horses will progress and then they often regress, too. It's fine. Just work with them at the level they're at instead of the level you want them to be. If they regress, go back to what you did before until they progress further.

One way to build confidence in a horse is by teaching them that they can make things move out of their way. For example, this horse was terrified of clippers, but if he could be convinced that he can push the clippers away from him, it would help eliminate some fear. So my next step was to do exactly that. I held the clippers up in front of my face,

turned them on, and started walking backwards. I pulled on the lead line
to encourage the horse to follow me. Every time the horse would take
a step forward, towards the clippers, I would turn them off and reward
him for the positive change. After just a couple of minutes doing this, the
horse was following me around the arena with no issues.

Now it was time for me to get a little more particular. I had been
pretty easy going up to this point. But now he was showing some real
signs of confidence around these clippers. I held the lead line and stood
about two feet in front of the horse. I turned on the clippers and quickly
put them up near his face and then quickly brought them back to my
side. He flinched a little, but nothing major, so I did it again. But this
time I left the clippers up near the left side of his face. He was still really
nervous, but he handled it. After a minute of the clippers being there, he
actually lowered his head slightly. I immediately turned off the clippers
for reward. Lowering his head was a form of relaxation and letting some
of that worry go.

RELAXED HORSE

Now it was time to actually let the clippers touch his head. But
before I get to that part of the story, I'm reminded of something very
important I need to point out here. Whenever you're trying to desensitize
a horse or get them used to being around a "scary" object, never ever do
anything slowly and creepy. When you move slow and creepy, it makes
the horse think that the object is a predator sneaking up on them. They
remain very unsure and bothered about it because they are wondering
if it's about to bite them, sting them, or hurt them in some other way.

Instead, use confidence and be firm. Act like it's no big deal and you do this every day.

When I finally let the clippers touch the horse's head, I turned them around backwards so that he could feel the vibration instead of the actual clippers. This was just another way to break something down into an easier step. Instead of going ahead and trimming some hair, I let him experience what the vibration felt like and let him get used to that. Then, once he tolerated that pretty well, I turned the clippers around and trimmed a perfect batch of hair out of his bridle path. The owner was stunned and exclaimed, "That's amazing".

It took about 40 minutes from the time we started until we finished. I didn't let her pay me the $100 because she agreed to let me film the whole thing for the Carson James membership website. It was a good trade.

CHAPTER 3
THE HORSE THAT RUSHED OFF THE TRAILER

BACKWARD FLYING HORSE

I got a call from a nice lady who was all concerned because she had a horse that would fly backwards off the trailer every time she tried to unload him. He would begin by taking a few steps back, which were fine, but then right before his back feet came out, he would really rush it. She was worried that the horse would end up hurting himself, or her, or both of them. So I told her to swing by the house and I'd take a look at the horse for her. I stood back and watched as she unloaded him and, sure enough, he darted backwards at full speed out of that trailer. Luckily she had a long lead line so she was able to feed it through her hand and still have a hold on the horse once he was out of the trailer.

In order to fix this issue, I needed to break down the elements of the trailer. Go into your horse's mind for a minute here. What are the elements of the trailer for a horse? He has to step up to get on, step down to get off, and then when he's inside, he's surrounded by walls.

I wanted to strip these elements down to their bare bones, so here's what I did. I got a pallet, put a rubber mat over it, and then began by getting the horse to step up on the pallet. He even had a hard time

doing this which led me to believe he also had problems loading, not just unloading. He would stand at the edge of the pallet while I was standing on the pallet and pulling the lead to encourage him to step up. He wouldn't budge. So I unlocked his front end by making him step to the right, then to the left, then back again, etc. But the whole time I kept the lead pretty tight which made him do the steps right in front of the pallet. Eventually he got pretty loosened up in his front end and put one foot

up on the pallet. I immediately rewarded him by releasing the pressure on the lead line and giving him a break. Long story short, we worked on this for a while, and I eventually got him with all four feet standing on the pallet.

Now I was finally able to actually start what I wanted to begin with. The step down from the horse trailer was pretty big, and it didn't have a ramp. So I wanted to work with the horse on the step down, but I wanted it to be less severe. Stepping backwards off a pallet would mimic the same movement as backing off the trailer, but the step down would be easier. Plus backing off of a pallet also eliminated the walls of the horse trailer. Working on the pallet, there weren't any claustrophobic walls around the horse which could have been adding to the issue. My goal was to get the horse to focus ONLY on stepping down without having any other elements involved. With both of us standing on the pallet, I held the lead and pushed him backwards to the edge. The foot stepped down. Good boy! I released the pressure and let him sit there

for a minute with that foot perched on the ground. Then I pulled the lead and encouraged him to step back up on the pallet. He did it. Good boy! Now let's do it again. Eventually he got really good at bringing that one foot down off the pallet and then back up again.

Now, just like in the example about the clippers, the horse was starting to "get it", so I started becoming a little more particular. This time, once the horse put one foot on the ground, I kept applying pressure until he put both back feet on the ground. One foot stepped back and I held steady pressure. Still nothing was happening. So I added a little more pressure and slightly increased it until that second back foot hit the ground. Good boy! I released all the pressure and let him stand there and reap his reward for a minute or two.

Another good thing about giving horses a break (reward) is that it gives them time to think and ponder on what just happened. A lot of times, when you're teaching a horse something new, you'll notice him licking his lips. This is a sign of contemplation. He's sitting there "chewing" on what he just learned and working it out in his head. After the break, I worked on this several more times until I felt like the horse had it down pretty well. It still wasn't perfect, but he had improved so much.

Now it was time for all four feet to come off the pallet and hit the ground. So, as you might guess, once the two back feet hit the ground, I kept consistent pressure until he started backing again. As soon as he started backing again, I stopped and gave him the reward. Then we backed up some more until one front foot came of the pallet. Good boy! I stopped, rewarded him, and gave him a minute to ponder. Then we started again and, after a few seconds, he had all four feet on the ground. I worked on this for a while longer until he was showing good signs of being comfortable with the whole exercise. One of the signs I noticed was that his leg movement was more fluid and he became less sticky. I wasn't having to use near the amount of pressure to get him to back off the pallet as I did when we first started. He was doing everything in one fluid motion and doing it faster, too.

Normally I would have wanted a few more days of "pallet work" on this horse, but he needed to go home that day, so we were on a time crunch. But I didn't want him to leave just yet. I asked the owner for just a few more minutes with the horse. She said that would be great.

I loaded the horse into the trailer and began doing the same exercise in the trailer as I did on the pallet outside. Except this time we were adding the walls back and we were increasing the distance of the step down. I began by pushing the lead line and asking him to take one step down. He did it, but you could tell he struggled with it a little more than he did on the pallet. That's fine and was to be expected. But the important thing here is that he actually did it. Good boy! I rewarded him and then pulled the lead to ask the back leg to step back up into the trailer.

Eventually we got the two back feet on the ground, and then all four feet. It was 10 times better than when she first arrived, but like I said, I would have wanted a few more days on the pallet before we started in the trailer. For the amount of time (less than an hour) that we worked together, you could see dramatic improvement. The horse was still "sticky" and unsure, but he wasn't rushing back and flying off the trailer. A few more days of pallet work, and a couple more inside the trailer would completely eliminate that problem. And that's exactly what I recommended the owner to do over the next several days.

CHAPTER 4
DUKE THE COCKY STUD

To understand how to help a horse, it is important to understand how horses help each other. Horses are made to be a certain way, and the closer you can simulate this "way", the better everything will be. From health to groundwork to riding, this helps your horse in every area of his life. The most important thing for a horse to have in the pasture, next to food and water, is a herd to live in. This is how they are wired to live. The horse's pasture mates do a substantial part in teaching order and respect. On the other hand, if you come across a horse that grew up alone, he may not even realize that leadership should and does exist.

Once there was a stud colt named Duke. He was sent for me to start and put the first 30 rides on. I had to leave town for a few days right after he arrived, but I got time to do a round pen session with him just before leaving. Duke was the prime definition of the typical stud colt. He was quite the handful. Duke had not the slightest idea of personal space and, of course, that also meant he was extremely inattentive and very full of himself -- not an ounce of humbleness to him.

When he was delivered to my place, the first night was spent in a stall. The next morning, after a short round pen session, I took Duke out to the pasture and turned him out with the other six horses. I had to go on a trip, and as I was packing to leave, all I could think about was

the work I had waiting on me when I returned. But it turned out that this was not the case at all. When I got home from the trip, I got him back in the round pen and started to do some simple groundwork. Boy, what a different horse! From that session, all the way up to his last day of riding, you would have sworn that he was a gelding. It was a complete 180 degree flip from the horse I left over the weekend. The other horses

HUMBLE

did in two days what would have taken me a week to do. They simply showed him that there were boundaries and rules that he had to operate within. They, for a lack of better words, put him in his place. They did all the work for me. Duke had never been raised in a herd, so he had no awareness of how the "real horse world" works. There had never been a bigger, dominant horse to pin his ears and cause Duke to yield and submit.

This is just one example of why, if possible, it's best to keep a horse in his natural herd environment. Sure, there will be times when you notice new scratches or bite marks from the horses picking at each other, but that is where we have to realize that this socialization is vitally important and that a horse needs it. We all want to care for our horses, but there is a fine balance between caring for them and getting in the way of nature. And, if we cross that line, we may very well be doing the opposite of helping our horses.

For all the years I've trained horses for people, I have always insisted that they allow me to run their horse in the herd. One big pot. However, in saying this, I want to stress that there are some cases where it can become too violent and could potentially cause a more severe injury than a simple knick or scratch. In a situation like this you would have to do something different. But for all the time I did this, constantly sending horses back to the owners and receiving new ones, I have never had to call a vet or doctor them for anything more than a scratch. If you had to choose between having some knicks every now and then, versus taking away the way he is supposed to live, I would choose the scratches. Mental soundness is just as important as physical soundness.

CHAPTER 5
THE "LAZY" HORSE

My buddy Dale asked me to work with one of his horses that he claimed was lazy. I didn't exactly know what he meant by that, so when he dropped the horse off at my place, I told him to hop up on his back and show me exactly what he meant by "lazy". As Dale started riding the horse around the arena, I knew exactly what the issue was. It wasn't so much that the horse was lazy. The horse didn't respond to leg pressure. Whenever Dale would ask him to get faster or try a little harder, the horse didn't amp up his speed or his energy. He just stayed at the same speed and energy level he was already at. Dale rode around the arena for a few more minutes, climbed off his horse, and handed him to me. He said, "He's all yours for the next two weeks while I'm out of town".

I was anxious to start working with this horse because I knew exactly what I could do to help him. All he needed was a better reason to respond to the leg pressure from the rider. At this point, leg pressure didn't mean much to him. So my job was to teach the horse that when he felt some pressure from the leg or a kick from the heel, that meant to speed up and try harder. To do this, I grabbed a little four foot riding whip out of my little barn. I climbed back on the horse and tapped him very lightly with the heel of my boot. As expected, there wasn't much of

a response. So I took the riding whip and tapped him firmly on the butt. That got his attention! He perked his head up and started walking with a brisk pace. Then we tried the whole process again. Although this time when I tapped him with my heels, his ears perked up a little bit. But he still didn't start moving. He was just standing there. So I spanked him again with the riding whip. That got his attention, and he started to walk off in a hurry.

Do you see what I'm doing here? I'm giving the horse the opportunity to respond to the light pressure of my heel tapping his sides before the heavier pressure of the riding whip comes. Whenever you're teaching a horse anything, you always have to give them a chance to respond to the lighter pressure first. Give them the opportunity, but if they don't take you up on that (the good deal) then you have to get firm and make it uncomfortable for them. In this case, I was making it uncomfortable for the horse to stand still.

By the third time we did this little training exercise, the horse began to walk when I tapped him with my feet. I worked with him like this for the next two weeks, and by the time Dale came back from his trip, he was a totally different horse. Now you could barely tap him on his sides and he'd trot right out nice and smooth. He learned that if he would respond to the lighter pressure first, that heavier, more uncomfortable pressure would never come. Dale was thrilled with the change and said he'd be send me some more to work on. It ended up being a good deal for me and the horse.

CHAPTER 6
AMBER AND THE BUDDY SOUR HORSE

I was at a local barrel race just hanging out and visiting with some of my friends. The event was almost over, and Amber walked over to me to see if I'd be willing to spend a few minutes working on her buddy sour (herd bound) horse. I didn't have anywhere else to be that day, so I told her I'd be happy to. Jared was there with me, so he grabbed the camera and captured it all on film for the membership site.

After we got the camera rolling, Amber explained to me that she had two barrel horses, and whenever she would ride either one of them, they would start acting up and fight her to get back to the other horse. Let's pause here for a minute. Why do you think that the horses liked being together? One reason was because whenever those two horses were together, they didn't have to do any work. Amber's horses were worked a lot because they were competing regularly at barrel races. Whenever she finished working the horses, she'd tie them up together, feed them, water them, and let them hang out. So the horses were associating being together as a better deal than working with Amber. The easier path, at this point, was to stand at the trailer and eat food. Our job, as horsemen, is to pave a different path.

So here's what I did. I told Amber to stand out in the middle of an open pasture and hold one of her horses. I got on the other one, crossed my arms, and made the horse start moving. I did nothing to steer him, I just kept him in motion. This horse was so buddy sour that he began doing circles around the other horse. So I amped up the speed (pressure), and made him work and work and work.

Eventually the horse decided he'd had enough of that, so he turned and began moving away from the horse Amber was holding (he made a change). What do you think I did at this point? I immediately stopped all of the pressure. I let the horse chill and relax. That didn't last

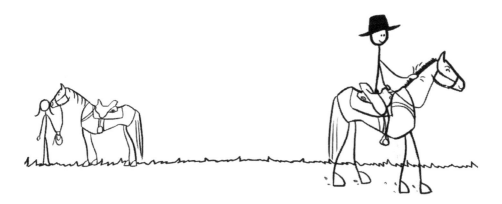

long. He decided he wanted to go back for some more. So as he started walking up to the other horse, I dropped my reins and amped up the pressure once again. Round and round we go! I just kept with it until the horse decided he'd try something else. As soon as he started to cut away (made a change) I let him relax and chill out.

It only took about twenty minutes for this horse to realize that whenever he was around his buddy he had to do a lot of work. It was much easier to stay on the other side of the pasture and relax. He didn't want to be anywhere near his buddy once we were through. I simply made the right thing (leaving the buddy) easy to do, and the wrong thing (staying near the buddy) more difficult to do.

You could do this exact same thing with a barn sour horse. If your horse is always wanting to rush back to the barn, then let him. But when he gets to the barn, don't take his saddle off and let him relax. Make him work when he gets back to the barn. Run him in circles, lunge him, or just do something. It really doesn't matter what you do as long as you're making the horse work. Pretty soon he will associate the barn with harder work and he'll quickly lose that barn sourness. It's all about making one option easy and making one option difficult.

CHAPTER 7
LEARNING TO STOP WITH HORSEY

Along time ago I was given a horse for free because no one else wanted him. He didn't have the best confirmation so people assumed he had no potential. The owner asked me if I would take him, and I agreed to do it. It took me a while to figure out the perfect name for this horse, but after a few weeks of pondering I ended up calling him Horsey.

One of the first few things I like to teach a horse is how to stop and slow down, mainly for safety. And just like any horse, Horsey didn't know that when I pulled back on the reins I wanted him to slow down or stop. He would run right through the pressure.

So, to help Horsey understand, here's what I did. I would get Horsey going, and then I would pull one of my reins so that it tipped his nose slightly (added pressure). This got in his way and made it

uncomfortable for him. He wanted to try to get out of that bind I put him in, so at first he kept trotting at the same speed. That didn't work for him. Then he tried tossing his head. That didn't work for him either. I continued to hold that bind, and then suddenly I felt him slow down a teeny little bit. I immediately dropped the bind and let him go. He stayed at that slower pace for a second, but then he started getting faster and faster. So I pulled one of the reins and tipped his nose again. He didn't immediately slow down, but it didn't take him near as long to figure it out this time. He slowed down slightly, so I released the bind.

What I was doing here is making it easy for him to slow down and making it uncomfortable for him to do anything else. He tried a bunch of different things to get out of that bind, but the key is that I didn't release the bind until he did what I wanted. Horses may try a lot of things to try and get out of the bind you put them in. Just ignore it and let them work it out. Only release when they make a positive change.

    Notice that I didn't wait for the horse to dramatically slow down or stop. I released when I felt his feet slow down just a tiny bit. Had I held that pressure after he began to slow down, that would not have taught him anything. He wouldn't have been able to connect that slowing down his feet was what caused that uncomfortable bind to go away. Once again, this is why timing is key.

I kept working with Horsey on this and, over time, I knew that he was starting to understand that pressure on the reins meant he needed to slow down, so I started to become more particular. I did the same thing as before and offered a little bind at first. But now, if his feet didn't immediately start slowing down, I pulled the rein harder (added more pressure) and put more of a bind on him. I gave him the opportunity to take me up on the good deal (the little bind) first. If he decided to delay his response, I amped up the pressure and his feet slowed down.

Fast forward to today and Horsey is feather light with his stops. As a matter of fact, he has a pretty good stop even bridleless. I had him with me on a ranch in Oregon and roped calves on him all day with nothing on his head. That was pretty fun. But it all started with making the right thing easy (slowing down) and the wrong thing difficult (not slowing down).

CHAPTER 8
THE HEAD TOSSER WHO WOULDN'T BACK UP

At one of the first clinics I ever did, I was nervous because I had never spoken in front of a lot of people before, let alone try to teach them something. We actually had a pretty good turnout, and it went really well. All of the participants ended up doing pretty outstanding, and there was one particular rider and horse that I will always remember.

Eva told me that her horse had a bad habit of tossing his head, so I asked her to show me. Every time she tightened the reins to try to get her horse to back up, he would fling his head up in the air instead. Obviously, the horse didn't understand that pressure from the reins meant he needed to move his feet. He thought tossing his head was the best way to get out of the bind he was being put in from the reins. And you know what? He was right. Why? Because every time he started his head tossing fit, Eva would release the bind. So, of course, the horse thought tossing his head was the answer. It gave him relief. At this point, I knew exactly what to do.

I told Eva to pull the reins back again, but this time don't let them go until the horse took just one small step back. As she pulled the reins, he began his head tossing fit, but Eva didn't give up. She held on

for a while, at least 10 seconds, until I looked down and saw one of the horse's back feet take a tiny step. "Release, Release!" I exclaimed. Eva sort of had a delayed reaction to my instruction. She was releasing the

pressure on the reins, but it wasn't fast enough. So I told her, "We are going to do this again, but this time I want you to drop your reins right when I tell you". She started again, pulling back on the reins, and as expected, the head tossing followed. I watched closely. As soon as I saw

one foot take a step back I yelled, "Drop 'em, Drop 'em!" This time Eva dropped the reins right away, and the horse immediately stopped tossing his head.

You see, by holding that bind through all of that head tossing junk, it's showing the horse that tossing his head is not the answer. It doesn't get him out of the bind. The horse needs to learn that the ONLY way to get out of that bind is to take one step backwards.

I told her if she'd just go home and work with her horse doing this exact same thing for the next week or so, it would pretty much eliminate the problem. I also explained that after the horse was starting to understand, she needed to get more particular. I suggested she could hold that bind a little longer until the horse got two steps instead of one. She'd basically be doing the same thing, but asking the horse to do a little more each time. If consistent, then the horse would learn how to back up with speed and a nice flow. Once again, it was the human that needed to make the adjustments, not the horse.

CHAPTER 9
THE HORSE THAT DIDN'T WANT ME ON HIS BACK

About 4 years ago I was sent this really nice colt to start and put the first 30 rides on. He was very well bred, smart, gentle, and very confident. After about 3 round pen sessions, he was moving nicely, turning in, and lunging at walk and trot in a halter. After that, I saddled him and sent him around a circle in the round pen about 5 times in each direction at a mixture between a trot, walk, and lope. He handled the saddle like it wasn't even up there.

The next day I started working on getting on his back. First, I put a halter on him, held the lead rope, and then put my toe in the stirrup. I hopped a few times and then laid across the saddle with with both legs hanging on the left side. As I pulled the lead out to the left, away from

his neck to untrack him (make his feet move), we had a lift off! He jumped forward into a buck, and I leaned back to slide off. When I hit the ground, I tripped and did a sideways somersault across the dirt. That didn't end very well, so something needed to change.

After he quit running around bucking, I got another hold of the lead, unsaddled him, and checked the pad and cinch for thorny type brusheries. Everything was fine. So I thought to myself, 'Well, let me take him through those few groundwork things again and see if I can hear him tell me something new.' He didn't say much of anything, so after a day of thinking, I finally thought, 'The groundwork is good. He didn't get the least bit bothered until I started to go up on his back.' So I saddled him again and used my hand to push down on the stirrup. He was perfectly fine with it. At this point I was stumped. I thought,

'Well, if it isn't saddle fit, respect, attention, or lack of confidence on the ground, then maybe he's getting bothered when I get above him.' So I decided to do a little fencing. Fencing is where you sit on the top rail of a fence or panel. You could also just stand on an object that elevates your body about three feet off the ground. The goal is to see how easily you can get a horse to give you his back. Giving his back is when he places his back directly underneath you, as if he were almost leaning up against the fence. He had some trouble with this, so the next two sessions we focused solely on fencing.

Now I could get him to very easily stand underneath me while sitting on the fence, and he would also let me swing a leg over, sit on him, and pet him all over his body. We went back to the center of the round pen, I laid halfway on his back again and untracked his feet with great success without an ounce of uncertainty. So I swung a leg over and within five minutes we were loping and trotting around the round pen without a single hiccup. Over the next 30 days, he even learned to stop and side pass. Needless to say, from that day on I fenced every horse that came to me, no matter how gentle he was.

What was confirmed from that experience is that there is a huge difference, to the horse, of being on the ground beside him and being above him. It's a whole different animal (no pun intended). Just because they are confident with a person on the ground, doesn't mean they are sure about said person being up above them, especially directly above their back. Even if you've been riding for years, you'd be surprised at the number of horses who can't do the "fencing" very well. Fencing really helped this horse get comfortable with me up there above his back. Before the fencing, he was bothered about me being up there, and that was the root of the problem which caused the symptom of bucking.

CHAPTER 10
THE EXPENSIVE HORSE THAT COULDN'T BACK OFF A TRAILER

Once there was this horse that had won upwards of $50,000 in the show ring, but could not back off of a trailer. You may be surprised to learn how common this type of thing is. The owner told me that he had several trainers try to work with this horse but with no success. If I were to name some of these trainers, you would immediately know who they are. And all of them had tried to get this horse to back off the trailer, but none of them could get it done. And by the way, I'm not telling you this story to sound boastful. I just want the reader to understand that the horse was obviously very far from being able to back off the trailer. It was a huge issue for him.

The owner said they had tried everything he could think of. But there was no way that they tried everything. The horse was still on the trailer! This was one of those times where I really needed to break it down for the horse, but, off the top of my head, I didn't know how. My horses had always just been able to figure it out.

So after contemplating for a few minutes I thought, 'Okay, maybe if I can get him to back down a hill it would help because that is similar to a ramp.' But I live in Florida and we don't have hills, so that complicated matters. I ended up finding of a dirt (okay, sand) mound. I tried to back him down this mound and sure enough he couldn't do it very well. "Ah Ha!," I said as the owner and several bystanders looked

at me as if I had lost my mind. "Yeah, but he's fine with backing down that hill, Carson," said the owner. And in a sense he was right, but there is a difference between doing something and doing it with sureness. The horse would take a few steps back, but then he would get crooked, step forward, or do something to evade backing down the hill. But about 15 minutes later, it got real clean and easy for the horse to back down the hill.

Next was backing into a stall. This was similar to a trailer because it was a big box type of opening, but the stall eliminated a good bit of the confinement factor because the walls were spread much farther apart than in a trailer. Although this horse had been led in and out of the stall for 15 years, he would not back into it. About the time he got close to the door of the stall, his hind end would pop over and avoid going inside. We continued to work at this and then, at around 20 minutes, he could do it clean and easy.

I had one more idea -- to find a shovel and scoop out some ground at the ledge of the stall where the concrete ended and the stall began. This would cause the horse to learn to take a step down as he was backing. After only 10 minutes, he had it! I could now stand a good 5 feet in front him and back him into the stall by simply shaking the lead a little.

Now it was time for real life. Back to the trailer we went. I led the horse up the ramp all the way to the front. It was a huge trailer pulled with a semi. I put my hand on the halter under his chin and began backing him with short releases of pressure between each step. For two minutes we took one step back, one forward, three back, two forward, one back and gradually worked our way to the ramp. Once at the ramp, I added some slight pressure again and boom! One back foot easily went back and landed on the ramp. Then two forward and three back. I took a minute to stop and pet him for a reward. I don't remember the exact amount of steps back and forth because it was a long time ago. If I had a memory that good I probably would have been a detective or something and this book would be about solving crimes. Anyway, where was I? Oh yes, the horse.

So now I had two hind feet on the ramp. From there we went all the way down the ramp and it was clean and smooth like he had done it a thousand times. Not once did he require more than a couple pounds of backing pressure on the halter. Me, the owner (and I'm sure the horse), were all amazed at how easy of a fix this was. In just under an hour, the horse was able to do something that had taken multiple attempts, and most of the horse's life, to try and fail. The moral of the story here is this: If you're having trouble with a horse, break it down and get those "pieces" of the bigger picture where they are good. That way, when the horse tries to put it all together, it won't be a blurry picture that is hard to figure out. Elementary, my dear Watson.

CHAPTER 11
THE GRASS LOVING HORSE

I was doing a clinic in the northwest, and a lady named Donna brought a horse that had a bad habit of constantly trying to eat grass anytime they were out trail riding. This had become such a major obstacle that her rides were no longer enjoyable. She was desperate to get this changed up so that she could once again look forward to going out riding with her friends. I quickly explained to her that there were a variety of 'issues' coming together to create this 'problem'. We needed to get to the root of the problem which would cause the symptom (eating on the trail) to disappear.

Before we started actually working with the horse, I knew that Donna first needed to understand some vital concepts. I told her to imagine she was sitting in her barn oiling her saddle and to really focus on that. I asked her to hold her hand out and then I used my hand to slightly push on her hand. It was pretty easy for her to ignore the pressure I was putting on her hand because it started out soft and only very gradually increased. When I realized she was not responding to that slight pressure, I quickly went from one ounce to ten pounds by suddenly pushing very firmly on her hand. That immediately got her attention, and it brought to mind the story about the boiling frogs. If you put a bunch of frogs in a pot of water but only gradually increase the temperature, they don't realize they're being cooked. But if you put them in a pot of boiling water, they'll immediately jump out. It's the same concept of being in a cold pool and then jumping into a hot tub. The temperature difference between the two waters would be extremely evident. But if you stay in the hot tub a while, you learn to 'wear' the heat, and it doesn't feel so hot anymore. You basically adapt to the 'pressure' of the hot water until it feels pretty comfortable, and it becomes easy to ignore the fact that you're sitting in hot water. A horse can also learn to 'wear' pressure so that it doesn't mean anything to him.

I wanted to make this super clear to Donna, so I pretended like I was her horse and I had a mouth full of beautiful, lush grass. Then, in the horse's voice of course, I said, 'Well, she's nagging me a little to lift my head, but I've still got a while before she really does anything about it, so I'll just keep eating and ignore her'. Then I explained that there's a difference in fixing it up and waiting for a horse to find it (as you would typically do for a colt) and holding them in a bind for 10 minutes while they're still pushing against it (which is typical of a horse that has learned to 'wear' pressure). You would need to do something to make it more uncomfortable because the horse has obviously learned to ignore pressure. This was the case with Donna's horse. As I say all the time, everything with horses in interrelated, so I was already convinced, without ever riding this horse, that it would take a good amount of pressure to get a response whether it was turning, backing, going, or stopping.

Donna hadn't owned the horse too long, but apparently the previous owners had essentially taught the horse to ignore them. He had also been taught that it's easier to push against the pressure than to yield to it. Remember that a horse never does right or wrong -- he does what, in his mind, is easiest. I knew the place to start was to set it up so that if the horse even began to attempt to push through pressure and try to eat the grass, he would suddenly run into a very large amount of pressure -- an immovable, invisible brick wall. A wall that he felt was self inflicted. To build this wall, we were simply going to absolutely prevent the horse from lowering his head down to eat grass. Because before a horse can eat grass, they have to lower their head, right?

We accomplished this by holding one rein and not allowing the horse to lower his head past a certain point. Using one rein takes away a lot of the horse's leverage. If you will notice, once you ever get the nose tipped just a little, it's much easier to bring their head on around. So I explained to Donna that one thing she should start doing is catching her horse right before he goes to reach for the grub. As soon as he goes for it, tighten up and hold firm on one rein. Don't jerk the rein, but hold it tight and don't let loose. That way when the horse goes down for the grass, he's going to run into all of that pressure. When he lifts his head back up after running into the pressure, then the pressure will automatically be released. This would help the horse to learn to stop reaching down for grass.

After that I thought of another method we could use to help Donna's horse. I had Donna start riding the horse around the arena. And, to make things interesting, I found a stash of fresh hay and put it right in his path. I told Donna, "You already know what's going to happen

when he gets to the hay, so be ready and catch it before he has a chance to commit to leaving you, both mentally and physically, and latching on to the hay. I had her walk some circles in the arena, and every time they came around to the hay, I'd have her bump him up into a trot. After they

were past the hay, I told her to bring him back to a walk and make things easy again. What we saw was that each time the horse got to the hay, it took less and less interference from Donna for him to get past the food magnet without thinking about trying to stop and eat it.

I then took on the role of the horse again to demonstrate WHY it's so important to get there early. I got on all fours, crept up to the hay, and completely buried my face in it. By then, I was committed to the food, ignoring everything around me. I explained again that before a horse does anything, he gets READY to do it. THAT is when you get there and help him take a different path. The sooner you get there, the less you have to do.

I knew I was getting somewhere when we brought the horse even closer to the hay, and Donna was able to recognize when the horse began to think about the food and intervene before he actually began going after it. It continued to take less and less from Donna to keep his attention off the hay because she had consistently made going for the hay difficult and going on past it easy.

One of the spectators brought up a good point. We had been using speeding up to get the horse past the hay, but you could really use anything --- turning, backing, flexing at the poll, etc -- to give him something else to think about.

To be effective in getting the horse's attention on something besides the hay, Donna also needed some help realizing the difference between pulling and bumping, so we made that clear. Bumping a rein is more effective and a lot harder to ignore than a steady pull when you're working to get the horse's attention. It's more fair to the horse to give him a chance to respond to light pressure and, if he doesn't, then amp it up to show him what you mean -- never abusively or above his level of understanding, but think back to the frog story. Donna's horse had learned to ignore pressure, so to get that changed up, the approach had to be modified. Continuing to beg him to respond, and not giving him a reason to respond, would not bring the changes she was looking for. To further illustrate the point, I began tapping Donna's leg. At first she was able to ignore it, but when I went from just a light tap to a hard tap, her toe moved. I made sure everyone watching caught the fact that as soon as her toe moved, the tapping stopped. As with everything,

the timing was critical. Then I went across the arena and told Donna that I was going to come up to her and hit her leg hard again if she didn't wiggle her toe and stop me. Anytime I walked toward Donna, she immediately wiggled her toe which kept me from coming up to her because I got the response I was after by simply turning towards her. Next, I walked right beside her and the horse, but she was not worried or anxious that I was going to tap her leg because anytime I began to reach for her leg, she wiggled her toe, which was the response I was after. There was no need to do more.

And just so everyone listening would not get the wrong idea, I had to make a disclaimer that if Donna's horse was a colt, I would probably not have used very much pressure at all to get his attention back to me. During our first time on the trail, if he tried to reach for food, a little bump from a rein or leg just few times would most likely get the job done. But since her horse had built up years of learning to ignore and push through pressure, it would take more pressure at first to get that changed around. The approach for Donna's horse versus the approach for a colt would be much different.

To finish out the session, and make sure Donna was confident in what we had worked on, I had her walk the horse around me in a circle on a loose rein. I told her that in 2 minutes she was going to ask the horse to stop. The main purpose of this was to more fully illustrate the amount of pressure to use and the timing of the release. Knowing that this horse was in the habit of ignoring and pushing through pressure, I reinforced the concept that she would ask with a light feel on the reins and quit riding with her body, and then if he didn't freeze in his tracks she would take ahold and have him back up five steps. He would run into that solid brick wall that was put in front of him by Donna's firm pull. As I expected, she asked him to stop, and he walked quite a few more steps before he came to a halt.

So then I once again pretended to be the horse and started trotting around. I had Donna whisper the word 'stop' but I ignored her and kept moving, so she said it louder -- 'STOP.' She didn't scare me, abuse me, or fail to give me a chance to stop with the whisper, but when I kept on pushing through what she was asking, she had to get firmer with her request. I stopped. The next time Donna whispered 'stop', I immediately came to an abrupt halt. Why? Because I was paying attention to her and listening for her request. I knew exactly what she was asking me to do because she had made it clear when she got firm with her earlier request. Her light whisper now went right down to my feet.

I was out of breath by then, but I had to make sure everyone understood that it's the approach you use that determines the result. For example, whether the horse ends up having a fear of the bit (head tossing, rearing, etc) or a healthy respect of the bit (lightness, softness). What did all these issues we worked on have to do with eating on the trail? Everything. Improving the attention, the amount of pressure, the timing of the release, the approach, even the stopping will come together to cause the horse to be more tuned in to the rider and less focused on what's around him, even when it's lush green grass.

Donna went home with a lot to think about and a lot to work on to help her horse. I felt confident that I had explained and demonstrated to the very best of my ability the concepts of horsemanship that she needed to know and put into practice to get the results she was wanting.

CHAPTER 12
SNUCKEL DUFFINS AND THE WATER HOSE

I ended up with yet another rescue horse, but this one didn't have a name. My wife, Brooke, wanted to name her, so I agreed. I was thinking she'd end up having a really cool or meaningful name, but I was wrong. Brooke named her Snuckel Duffins. "Are you serious?" I asked her. "YES!", she exclaimed. So Snuckel Duffins it was. Snuckles (nickname) had the absolute best horse life. I was busy training other horses, so I didn't have much time to work with her. She got to just graze out in the pasture, eat grain, and basically do nothing. She had it made.

Then one day we decided we were going to use her as a demonstration for a video on one of my DVD's. The problem was that she was filthy. So I put a halter and lead on her, took her up to the water hose, started spraying water at her (added heavy pressure), and she started freaking out. She was snorting, blowing, tossing her head -- the whole nine yards. I told my brother, Jared (he films the videos), that we should just do a video on desensitizing to water instead of what we were going to originally film. What a great opportunity!

The key here, just like everything else, is to break it down. The hose going full blast at her body was too much for her to handle, so I started out with my back turned to her and very gently squeezed the nozzle of the hose to let out a light stream of water (light pressure). I was holding the hose out in front of me so the water was shooting away from Snuckles. Just doing that was enough to get her bothered. She wasn't bothered as bad as when I sprayed the hose at her full force, but she was still ancy and snorting at the water.

If the horse was already bothered at this point, then it would be safe to assume that she'd be even more bothered if I turned around and started spraying her, right? That's why reading your horse is so

important.   You must work where the horse is at, and
only do as much as they can handle. If your horse gets a little bothered,
that's ok. But don't try to progress past that point with more pressure
until they're comfortable with the current amount of pressure you're
using. The key is simply breaking it down and fixing each piece in
increments.

Once Snuckles calmed down and seemed like she was handling
the water being sprayed away from her, I began moving the water closer
to her. I simply backed up a few steps and then sprayed the nozzle out to
the left side of my body and the right side of my body. So instead of the
water going directly away from her, it was now spraying at a 90 degree
angle. She had been moving all around and snorting, but for a second
she calmed down and relaxed. At that point, I turned the water off.

CALM SNUCKLES

This was helping her learn that the way to make the water go away is to relax.

After a few minutes I began to amp up the pressure a little bit. I turned around and started spraying the water in front of her feet. Some of the water was even bouncing up off the ground and getting her front feet a little wet.

Whenever a horse realizes that they can move something out of the way, it increases their confidence. So my next step was to continue spraying the water at her feet, but then put some pressure on the lead line to encourage her to step forward. As soon as she stepped forward, I turned the water off. What I was having Snuckles do is the opposite of what a horse normally does, which is to try go get away from something they're afraid of. That's why it's so important to understand that when they start to move around a little bit, and you're trying to get them used to something, you don't allow them to get away from it. Yes, you do want to allow your horse to move her feet, but when your horse does move her feet, you go with her. That way the horse still has their self preservation and flight instinct intact, but they don't feel confined. But, at the same time, you're not letting them find a release by moving their feet to get away from whatever you're trying to get them desensitized to. It's also important to make sure you're not adding more pressure than the horse is ready for. You must smart small, get them used to it at that level, and then begin adding more.

In this case, it was now time to amp up the pressure a little more. Instead of just asking for one step forward towards the water, I asked for

2 or 3 before I turned off the hose (released the pressure). She handled that pretty well, so I decided to take it a little further. She was already becoming okay with the water hitting her feet, so I started at her feet and slowly worked my way up her body to the base of her neck. She stood there very calm, so I turned off the water and gave her a pat on the head (rewarded her).

After that, I began spraying her back feet and she started moving around a little bit which let me know that was bothering her. But I didn't stop spraying. I kept going until she stopped moving around. Once she stopped moving, I turned off the water and gave her a minute to think. I could see her chewing and licking her lips, so I knew she was thinking hard on what was happening.

Now, if I had just held Snuckles lead tightly where she couldn't really get away from the water and move her feet, what do you think would have happened? It would have been a huge blow up! It doesn't matter what you're doing, you always have to give horses a way to release the pressure. And you do that through the feet. It's vital that a horse can freely move their feet.

I went back to spraying the front feet and worked my way up higher and higher to where I could now spray her down the side of her

body and down her back without her being very bothered. Most of the time she would stand there pretty calmly and let me spray her. So I worked with her about 15 more minutes and was able to work my way up her neck and eventually wash her face. We got it all on film.

CHAPTER 13
THE BARREL HORSE THAT COULDN'T SLOW DOWN

Many horses that are professional athletes, specifically barrel racing horses, tend to always want to go. If you've ever ridden a horse like this, then you know how aggravating it can be. Levi was a prime example of a horse that thought he always had to go fast. He had won some money, and was on his way to being a pretty great barrel horse, but it was impossible to just ride him around on a loose rein. He was sent to me for a tune-up, and one of the things I immediately noticed was that he always wanted to be out in front of me when I was riding him. Every time I'd get up on his back, he would start walking fast and eventually break into a trot.

There's a couple of ways I decided to work on this to help the horse understand. The first thing I did was bump a little on the right rein. I would pull the rein lightly then let off, then pull lightly again, then release. This caused some pressure in the corner of the horse's mouth and made it uncomfortable for him. I just kept doing this until I felt his feet slow down. As soon as his feet slowed down, I stopped doing it. He didn't understand at first, and kept walking in that really fast pace. But I

was persistent and kept making that uncomfortable for him. After about 15-20 minutes, he started to figure out that in order for that annoyance to stop, he had to slow down his pace.

Once again, this is why timing is critical. Had I stopped doing the little bumps before or after he slowed down, he wouldn't have understood that slowing down was what caused the bumps in the rein to go away. It was crucial that my release of pressure (the bumps in the rein) happened the very second I felt those feet slow down.

Another thing I did was attempt to redirect his energy. So instead of just letting him walk in a straight line, I started making him work and do some tight figure eights. I let all of that energy he had be drained out

through his feet by doing some hard work. After a few minutes he started slowing down, so I let him relax walk in a straight line. Then he started going fast again, so I redirected the energy back to those figure eights. Within just a few sessions of this he started learning that whenever he sped up it meant he had to do those direction changes again which were a lot harder than walking in a normal, straight line. I was simply making it easier for him to walk at a slow pace and more difficult to walk fast or trot.

After about a week of doing these little exercises, the problem was totally cured. I could now ride Levi on a loose rein, and he would hang his head and relax. In fact, Levi got so good that I could drop the reins and ride him with my arms crossed. Those were just two of many methods that could have been used, but those particular methods worked very well to help him. That's why I stressed in chapter 1 that it's not WHAT you do, it's HOW you do it. The timing of the adding and releasing pressure is what did helped this horse to understand.

CHAPTER 14
THE HORSE WITH BRIDLING ISSUES

A while back, a lady named Kate called me because she was having a terrible time getting her horse bridled. She asked me if she could bring the mare to my place for some help. When she arrived, she explained that the horse was getting increasingly worse about bridling, throwing its head and jerking away to the point that it had now become dangerous. When we started working with the horse, it became apparent that a lot of the problem was that she was really sensitive about anything being close to her ears. She was better if you approached her ears from the front, but very bothered about her ears being approached from the back. I told Kate that the key to getting her past this issue would be to use good timing and to be aware of the smallest change. To better show her what I meant, with the horse in a halter and me holding on to the leadrope, I placed my hand on the horse's poll. That caused her to try to pull away from me and throw her head up, but I just hung in there with my hand on her poll until she slightly relaxed more about it. Her eye softened and her head lowered just a bit. As soon as that happened, I took my hand down. Notice here that I only gave a release of pressure (my hand going away)

when she began to relax. The next time I put my hand on her poll, she did the same thing --- jerked her head up and attempted to pull away. So I left my hand up there until she softened, which happened a little quicker than it did the first time. I immediately took my hand down. I explained to Kate how important it was to hang in there with my hand on the mare's poll until we got a change. Otherwise, we'd be rewarding the horse for jerking her head away.

Another important thing to remember was that I didn't do more than she could handle. I told Kate, "I'd love to be able to just reach up there and rub all over her ears right now, but that would turn into a wreck, and she'd probably end up dragging me all over the yard. That's why we're breaking this down and doing little bits at a time." We were trying to get the horse to be able to take more, but we didn't want to cross the line that the horse had drawn. Our goal for now was to move that 'line' further up without causing a big fight or make the horse feel like she had to defend herself.

We did this for the next little while, but now it was time to add some more pressure. So instead of just placing my hand on her poll, I moved my hand around and started rubbing her poll. She was a little bothered at first -- her ears were back and she was somewhat tense -- but it wasn't more than she could tolerate. Any time she softened, of course, the rubbing stopped and my hand was removed. We went back and forth gradually increasing and releasing pressure for a few more minutes, but I made sure to never ease off until there was a positive change. I explained to Kate that if I just kept rubbing and rubbing without releasing the pressure to reward the change, the horse would never learn that the way to make the pressure go away is to yield to it instead of fight against it.

To move that 'line' the horse had drawn a little further up, now when I was rubbing her poll, I also used my thumb to touch her ear. She was a little troubled by it at first, and shook her head to try to get rid of me, but I hung in there until she relaxed about it some. Since this horse was so bothered about her ears, if I had started out trying to stroking the ear right at first, without the work we had done by just touching and then eventually rubbing the poll, that would have been too much for the horse to handle. But now she was ready to tolerate a little more. I also pointed out that I wanted the horse to realize that she could actually control what I did by what she did. If she accepted me rubbing her ear, the rubbing would stop.

It had only been about 10 minutes since we first started, and we were already seeing a lot of progress. I told Kate to always be looking for positive changes -- in this case, lowering the head, a softer

LOWERING HEAD   SOFT EXPRESSION   LICKING LIPS   TAKING A BREATH

expression, licking the lips, taking a breath -- anything that indicated she was 'turning loose', both mentally and physically. Rewarding those changes will build the horse you DO want instead of the horse you DON'T want.

About then, Kate asked if you would want to do the same things on both the right and left sides. Glad she brought that up. I moved to the other side and began doing the same things continuing to look for a good place to reward her tries. Just because a horse is getting more sure about something on one side of their body, doesn't mean that they are sure about it on the other side. So we continued to play the game of give and take, hot and cold, for another 10 minutes. The 'line' had moved up quite a bit to the point where I could rub the front and back of her ears without much resistance.

When the mare put her ears up to notice another horse out in the pasture at the same time I was rubbing her ear, I knew we were getting somewhere. She was beginning to basically ignore the fact that my hand was all over her ear and was able to focus on something else (the other horse). A huge improvement from where we started 20 minutes earlier when she wouldn't let you anywhere near her ear. I wanted to make sure Kate understood that though we had gotten the ear 'issue' a lot better, she would need to continue to work on it until the horse was consistent and confident about it. Then the horse you want is right on the surface, and you don't have to dig around for it like we had done today.

CHAPTER 15
THE HORSE THAT BUCKED AND BOLTED

I have received countless emails that start out the same way. They go something like this: "I was out riding my horse the other day, and then out of nowhere, he just started bucking." The first thing you should realize is that nothing with a horse is ever "out of nowhere". Your horse will give you little signs (like we talked about in chapter 1) that will clue you in on potentially bigger problems. If a horse is never (or rarely) allowed to go faster than a walk, and always held back, they're like a pressure cooker waiting to blow. That steam builds and builds until one day it explodes. Horses need to be allowed to let those feet move with some life so they can release their pressure instead of storing it up until the day it all releases at once.

One of the first things that I do with my colts is get them up into a lope and moving their feet. This gets the horse used to some speed so whenever they do have to get faster, they aren't unsure about it and are able to handle it. It's the same when a horse gets spooked. Let's say a squirrel hops in the bushes on the trail, and your horse interprets the squirrel as a big, scary monster. If he gets startled and speeds up, and he's not used to speeding up, he could bolt, buck, or worse.

A group of friends hired me to do some lessons with them at the arena near my house. One of the ladies in the group told me that her horse would occasionally bolt or buck if he ever sped up or got spooked.

So I asked her how often she rode the horse faster than a trot. She told me that she had only done it on a few occasions. I knew right away that this was the problem. The good news about this is that it's an easy fix, but the human, as usual, has to get out of the horse's way.

I asked her to ride out across the arena just so I could see how she was riding her horse. I noticed that every time the horse started to speed up she had a habit of reaching down, grabbing the reins, and

pulling on the horse to get him to slow down. Not good. So I closed the gates in the arena and told her to cross her arms and just ride. She was not allowed to reach down unless I said so. And she couldn't do it. She was so terrified of going much faster than the speed she was accustomed to that she couldn't keep her arms crossed. I explained to her that if she didn't trust me, and get this resolved, she would be riding a very unsafe horse which could cause her to get hurt.

After a few minutes, she slowly but surely kept her arms crossed longer and longer until the horse made it up into a lope. Once her horse began loping, I told her she could put her arms down, but to try not to pull on the reins. If the horse kept speeding up, she could tip the nose to slow him a little. She ended up doing a great job and made a couple of laps around the arena at a lope. Both her and the horse's confidence got a huge boost that day.

Before she left, I reinforced how critical it was that this became part of her every day riding regiment. I also reminded her that since they were both new to this, she needed to begin in a controlled environment like an arena or round pen before riding on a trail or anywhere else. I wouldn't suggest taking any horse out on the trail until he can walk, trot, and lope on a loose rein. Only then is he ready to handle the uncertainties that may pop up.

CHAPTER 16
TRAILER LOADING AT LIBERTY

My buddy Jimmy lives up the road from me. He trains horses too, so we often ride and hang out together. I wanted to do a video demonstration for the Carson James member website, and I asked Jimmy if he had any horses that didn't want to load in the trailer. He told me he did, so Jared (my brother) and I grabbed the camera, hopped in the truck, and headed over there. I wanted to show how you could train a horse to load in a trailer at liberty, without using a halter or lead rope.

I built a round pen out of panels that were lying around and left an opening where I could connect the 2-horse straight load trailer to the panels. I try to use a small trailer for demos because, as a general rule, if a horse will load easily in a small trailer, a bigger trailer will be a piece of cake. So we backed the trailer in and tied the panels off to each back door. I lead the horse into the round pen and then let him go. I got a lunge whip with a plastic bag tied to the end of it and added a little pressure to cause the horse to start trotting around the pen. When he would make his way around to the opening where the trailer was, I'd stop waving the bag and relax (released the pressure). Then when

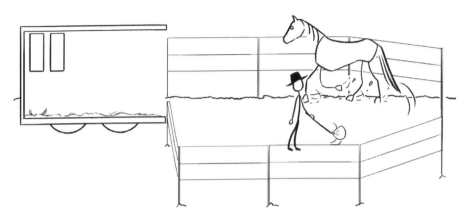

he'd leave that area and walk to another part of the pen, I heated up the pressure again and made him work. This horse ended up being good to use for the video (we like to use real life examples and not horses that already know what to do) because he was obviously very bothered at the beginning, but before long he decided that staying down there by the back of the trailer was a pretty good place to be. He didn't have to work and he could just chill out.

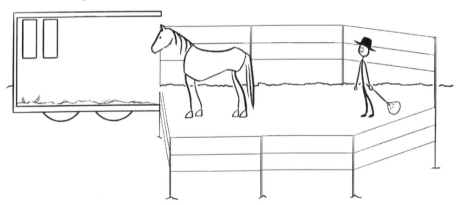

After he got to where he would stand by the trailer, I began to get more particular. I lightly waved the whip, just enough to get his attention, but not enough to make him move from where he was at. The light wave of the whip was more than enough for him to start paying attention. Every time he'd look at me, or at anywhere else besides the inside of that trailer, I'd put some light pressure on him. Then when he looked in the trailer, I'd immediately stop waving the plastic bag and let him rest.

Now it was time for phase two. I wanted him to put one or both of his front feet in the trailer. So I amped up the pressure a little bit, and he started running around the pen. It was fine though. He just

didn't understand. We tried it again once he stopped by the trailer. But this time he reached down and sniffed the inside of the trailer. That was a sign of positive change and something he hadn't done before, so I let that be a reward for him. I allowed him to stand there and sniff the

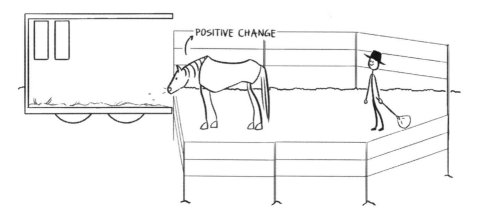

trailer for a while. Then he turned his head out of the trailer and started paying attention to the horses in the pasture beside us, so I amped up the pressure again by waving the whip. This caused him to turn into the trailer and put his front foot inside of it. I immediately dropped the pressure and let him stand there with his foot propped. He started to back out, so I added a pretty good amount of pressure which caused him to stop backing up and actually put another foot inside.

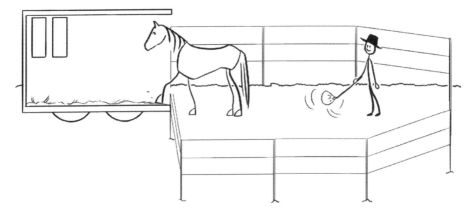

This is the point where people mess up with trailer loading. Once the horse starts moving inside the trailer, many people want him to finish getting in, so they add a lot of pressure on the horse while he's doing something positive. Do you see how this is the direct opposite of what needs to be done? If you add pressure to the horse when he's doing what you want, you're teaching him to stop doing what you want. The time to add pressure to the horse is NOT when he's going forward into the trailer.

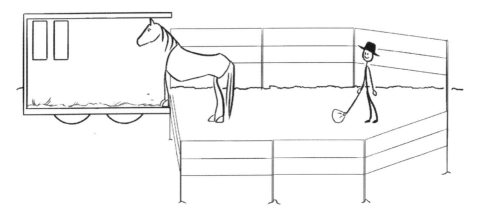

So now the horse was standing there with both front feet inside the trailer and both back feet on the ground. I let him stand there for a while and have a good amount of release. Then I added a little more pressure and he backed out. That's ok. I just made him do a few laps around the round pen at a pretty hasty pace. Then I let him stop again once he got back around to the trailer. I made it difficult on him for backing out of the trailer by making him run around a few times.

Alright, time to go to phase three now. I knew that the horse was getting comfortable with putting his nose in the trailer and his two front feet, so I got even more particular. I put some pressure on him by waving the flag and he almost immediately stepped both feet into the trailer. I gave a very short release but then added some pressure again pretty soon after that. One of his back feet moved towards the trailer. What do you think I did? I stopped all the pressure and let him stand there for a second. Then I just came right back in and added some more pressure until I got another step. Pretty soon (about 40 minutes) of playing this game of hot and cold with the horse, I got him fully loaded.

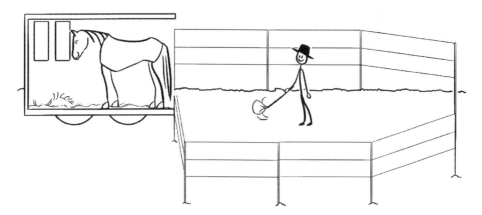

In fact, it made Jared and I start laughing because then we couldn't get the horse out of the trailer when it was time to leave. I had made him so "barn sour" to the inside of that trailer that he was perfectly content to stay in there. We kept working with it and eventually got him out. It made a killer video.

CHAPTER 17
THE REARING HORSE

I was doing a Vaquero Horsemanship demonstration at Horse Fair when I met Amy. She had a horse that had developed a bad habit of rearing, especially when she was asking him to back up. Apparently, he had even reared straight up a few times which can be extremely scary and dangerous. We've all heard those horror stories about a horse rearing up and falling over on the rider, many times resulting in a tragic loss. I sure didn't want this to happen to Amy, so we met up at the round pen to see if I could help figure out WHY the horse was rearing, which would be the key to getting him to stop feeling like that's what he needed to do. The headgear Amy had for the horse was a shank bit with a curb chain. I explained to her that with a leverage bit like this, she may only be applying three ounces of pressure, but the horse is feeling much more. So it's hard to gauge the correct amount of pressure to use, not really knowing how much pressure the horse is feeling on the other end. If the horse was backing really well already, the leverage bit might be fine, but with the issues he was having, it was definitely the wrong gear to put on his head. Luckily, I had a few traditional hackamores with me, so we put the leverage bit aside and used the hackamore on the horse.

Amy and I had already talked about how important it would be to free up the horse's feet. If a horse is free in his feet, he's free in his mind. I explained to her, and the crowd that had gathered to watch --- "A horse that gets locked up and feels sticky would be the same horse that would rear. For a horse to rear, his back feet are braced, and his way of 'escape' is to pop up in the front." I had Amy jump on the horse as I reminded everyone how critical it is that a horse can be ridden on a loose rein. Over time, if you're constantly holding the horse back, trying to contain that excess energy, it will build and build until one day, it will explode. Amy had never ridden in a hackamore/mecate rig before, but she was sure willing to try it to help the horse get past the rearing issue.

Before I let her walk off, I went over the importance of rein management. I told her to be sure her hands were wide, forward, and low. The reason was that if she asked him to turn, but also had back pressure on the rein, he would feel trapped which would bring on a possible rear. But if her hand was out to side and forward to lead him into a turn, the horse would not feel closed off in the front and would be free to just follow right around.

I had her start walking the horse around the pen on a loose rein and then turn him to bring him towards me. With her guiding hand low and forward, the horse easily turned without any trouble. I told her that if he did try to go up into a trot, to not just cut him off, but to redirect his feet until he came back down to a walk.

I wanted to start working on getting the horse to turn loose in his hind end, so I had Amy turn the horse's nose to the left, but at the same

time use her left leg to push the hind end away. He wanted to speed up, so I had her turn the nose more to the left while continuing to use her left leg to ask his hind end to step over. He was a little braced in his neck at first, but as we continued this exercise his neck loosened up. I had her maintain the bend, and then use the left rein to almost stop the front end while at the same time bringing her left leg slightly back to see if she could push the hind end over. I stepped in and added a little more pull to the rein, and the hind end stepped around. Now Amy knew what that felt like and what we were looking for. We were beginning to bust loose all the tightness that had been contributing to the rearing and, so far, both front feet had stayed on the ground.

We changed it up and did the same exercise to the right. Then I had her ask him to back up. She was a little apprehensive because of the rearing in the past, but I assured her that we would not make the horse feel like he had to rear to escape the pressure. I had her gather up the reins and hold pressure asking him to back until his weight shifted and he took one step. At that instant, I said 'Release him', which she quickly did. I had her continue to swing in with pressure and then fully release

every time he took a step back. She did a good job with her timing and the horse didn't seem at all bothered. So then I asked her to do that same thing with pressure and release, but this time only slightly release, and then come back in with pressure to ask for another step back. I watched the horse's feet and helped Amy know when to apply back pressure and when to release. So far, the horse had not been sticky and everything was flowing pretty smoothly. Everytime he moved a foot back, he was feeling a release, so there was no reason to look for another way out (rearing). I told Amy that the horse would back up as easy as he would rear. Our job was to make backing up easier than rearing --- fix it up and let him find it.

For the next exercise, I explained to Amy how it's hard to direct something that's not already in motion. It's much easier to turn the steering wheel on a car that's moving than it is on one that's sitting still. For the same reason, I asked her to get the hind end stepping around, draw with her reins, and release when the hind foot reached back instead of forward. The point was to teach the horse to stay fluid and flowing and not lock up in his hind end. Fortunately, Amy could feel the difference when the horse really reached with his hind foot, so she had

a reference point to know when to release. So we continued doing this on both sides for a few minutes. The horse was beginning to turn loose physically and mentally and had still not offered to rear one time. Amy had done a good job, but I wanted to get on the horse to further demonstrate the process of how to quickly get a horse to know that the release from pressure is always through yielding his feet --- not through tossing his head, bolting, freezing up, or rearing. So she hopped off, and as I was getting on the horse, I pointed out that not one time had the horse been locked up. Some of the reason was that we switched the headgear, and some of it was the way we presented what we were asking. To this point, the 'rearing horse' had not reared, but it was because we had never made the horse feel like it HAD to rear to escape the pressure. A horse that rears thinks the release comes from rearing, and a horse that backs up lightly and consistently thinks the release is through backing up.

PRESSURE RELEASE:

REARING HORSE   BACKING-UP HORSE

I continued to work on freeing up the hind end and reinforcing that the way out of pressure was to yield his feet. He continually got more fluid and smooth in his movements. Any time he wanted to speed up, I tipped his nose until his feet slowed. Before long, he quit trying to be out in front of me because he had been given a reason to NOT be out in front of me. As I continued to also work on backing, I only slightly released with each step, and before long he was backing across the pen with little effort from me.

More folks had gathered up to watch, so I took that opportunity to explain that if a horse thinks he can't escape pressure, he'll fight it. So it's up to us show him there is a way of escape. The obvious changes in this horse after only 30 minutes was a perfect example. He no longer deserved the title, 'The Rearing Horse'.

CHAPTER 18
STORIES FROM COW CAMP
JIM AND THE TWO HORSES

I spent a couple of years in the high desert of Oregon doing some cowboy work on a pretty massive ranch. My friend/co-worker Sam and I had been working hard, and we were pretty caught up on everything. The next day, the boss explained that during the next week, we were supposed to start a bunch of different horses. Our reward for being caught up? These horses were all penned together in the corrals, and a few of them were 4 year olds, a couple were 3, and the rest were upwards of 5 years old. Most of them were almost completely unhandled by humans.

Now before I go any further into this story, I have to tell you about Jim. He was another guy on the cowboy crew at the ranch and one of my superiors, I think. It was really up in the air if Jim actually had any authority, although I think he did. He is much easier to explain in person, but I'll try to describe him on paper because this story is much better once you know a little about him. He was a real nice guy, pretty stocky, and probably in his late 50's. He had somewhat of a lisp when he talked, and he always brightened the day. He was also pretty handy with horses and sat on a horse real nice (he was a good rider with a nice, natural posture). He was also very funny, but he didn't know he was funny because he always took himself pretty serious. He wore glasses, and whenever he would remove his glasses, his eyes would go crossways.

Okay, back to the story now. After we had been given our new assignment, Jim stopped by the corrals, peered into the herd and said with his signature lisp, "Hey you guys -- see that bay and that roan standing there? Those are two older ranch horses that jumped the fence

a few years back and got into the mountain pasture with those stud colts. They've been ridden a bunch in the past. Turn the other horses out tonight, but leave those two penned up so you can use them to gather the horses again on Monday morning." Sam and I assured Jim that we would do that, and then headed to town for the weekend.

We had a large time in town and pretty much spent our entire month's wages on silver bits and rawhide reins. Sunday night, we got back to headquarters and we were both broke, but we had some nice new bits. Jim walked up and had a new word from the boss. He said, "Hey Carson, the boss says that there's about 20 cows in the pasture just north of the corrals, and their water is drying up. He wants you and Sam to use those two horses you left penned in the corrals to go gather the cows and move them to the next pasture north. Once you finish that, you can get back to your colt starting."

So we came back to the corrals Monday morning and tried to catch the two horses to saddle them. It took a while to even get them caught, and we ended up roping one of them. Normally this would have

been a red flag warning, but these were ranch horses. Plus they had been out in the wild for the past several years, so we figured they'd just gotten a little rusty. We ended up hobbling their two front feet in order to saddle them. Normally this would have also been a red flag, but these were ranch horses. We figured with how things had gone thus far, it would be smart to run them around the corral for a lap or two. They bucked pretty good, then bucked a little less, but never got completely normal. Usually this would have been yet another red flag, but these were ranch horses.

After another 5 minutes we had to get going because it was getting late in the morning. Sam and I led our horses out the soft powered dirt road that goes out of the corral gate and into the pasture where the cows were. We went to mount, and right when Sam got his leg swung over, his horse started to buck. He rode it out and managed make it a few hundred feet down the road. My horse began walking towards Sam and then randomly started trotting for about 10 feet. He then burst into bucking still headed towards Sam. He bucked for what seemed like forever, and all I could see was dust and my saddle horn. Sam told me later that all he could see was my hat going up and down then up then down. I managed to stay on and we finally started trotting to where we

thought the cows might be.

As we trotted, we tried to make a slight course correction, and it was real strange. The horse's heads went straight up, and it felt like all four feet were trying to go in different directions. "Man, whoever started these horses was a sorry hand," I said to Sam. He agreed. Then he informed me that his horse didn't have any woah. I told him mine was the same. The only thing we could do is sort of tip their noses to the side a few inches, and this would slow them up just a hair.

Then we came up on a ditch that our horses leaped over, and as soon as those front feet hit the ground -- Kaboom! They both blew up and started bucking again. I got bucked off pretty bad, and it knocked the wind out of me. Sam stayed on his. He was a lot better bronc rider than me. As the day went on, they never bolted on us, but all together we each went for about 4 different bronc rides. But after those 4 episodes, I guess they got it all out of their systems because they never bucked anymore after that. We ended up getting the cows moved, but man was it a pain in the butt and took way longer than it should have.

Sam and I returned to the corrals around 4 p.m. and had enough time to handle a few colts before going back to headquarters. Jim stopped in at the end of the day to see if we gotten the cows on fresh water, and we told him how the day went. He began peering back into the herd again, this time with his glasses on, and got a very surprised look on his face. "What is it, Jim?" I asked. Insert lisp here --- "Man, I'm sorry you guys. I didn't have on my glasses the other day. Those aren't the two horses I thought they were," Jim explained. "What do you

mean?" asked Sam with a extremely irritated look on his face. Jim then informed us that he was mistaken -- the bay and roan he had told us to ride had never even been halter broke.

That's the day I was forever convinced that it's much better to take the time to get the horse where it needs to be before you get on him and expect things to go smoothly. Sam and I could have spent an extra 30 minutes before heading out that morning and saved at least that much time by not having to go in random directions and ride out the bucking fits. That day I also learned not to rely on Jim for a visual profile of a horse -- unless he had on his glasses.

CHAPTER 19
PICKING UP THE RIGHT LEAD

T here was a man who called and said that his horse refused to pick up the right lead. He had taken him to a lot of trainers, yet no one was able to help this horse. A few days later the owner showed up, and I asked him to demonstrate what his horse had been doing. The first thing I noticed is the horse could not really trot. The second thing I noticed was, because of that, he would go from a slow, bound-up trot to popping on up into the lope without ever extending his stride. This is where the root of the problem was. The horse was not preparing to lope. He was just doing it. Before a horse does anything, they need to prepare to do it. Out in the pasture he didn't have any trouble picking up the right lead, but that was because there was not a human to get in his way. There is a very fine line between operating the horse and staying out of his way at the same time.

So once I got on, the first thing I did was adjust the reins so that the instant he started to try to lope, I could get in his way, and then release when he would go back to trotting. It took about 15 laps around the arena, but he eventually could extend his trot and hold it. After some

practice, the rider can acquire the ability to feel, from the extended trot gait, when the horse is and is not in a body position to pick up the correct lead.

This horse's body position was a 'no go' at almost every point in the arena except for one sweet spot at the northwest corner of the arena. This is pretty typical for horses that have this issue. So when I came upon that sweet spot, at the northwest corner, I rode a little faster, and he extended the trot a hair more. By now the horse was trotting about as fast as he physically could without loping.

The second time we came around and started getting in the northwest section, I rode a little faster, but I didn't actually try to kick the horse up into the lope. That would have messed it up. I just put some life in my body and posted the trot with a bit more energy. Voila! The

horse rolled very smoothly up into a lope and was on the correct lead. He didn't need help picking up the right lead. He just needed help preparing and getting his body in the correct position to do it. But he had not yet realized that's what I was after. So we rested for a couple minutes, and then started trotting around the whole arena again. But this time, when we got to that northwest corner, and I felt his body get "right," I eased off and we stood still for a minute or two. That was the reward. This was teaching him that this is what I was wanting him to do -- get in the correct position to pick up the right lead.

So we kept working on that a few more times, and after about five more laps, the horse started getting "right" at different parts of the arena. Every time I felt that right lead body position begin to come, we stopped and rested. After another five minutes, that good position showed up and held for the three entire laps around the arena, and then we rested.

At this point I told the owner, "Ok, come give it shot. Don't think about loping. Think about trotting faster and faster and faster, and once you max out the trot, the horse will think, 'Well I can't trot any faster, I've got to lope.' Once they did that, he was able to pick up the correct lead at all sections of the arena. Since then I've done this with hundreds of horses that would not pick up the correct lead and it has worked within 10-20 minutes every single time.

CHAPTER 20
THE HORSE THAT RAN SIDEWAYS

About a year ago we were doing a clinic in Arizona, and there was a horse that was real bothered by all of the other horses going by him. At clinics, sometimes I'll have all the riders go in a big circle the same direction around the arena on their horses. Every time a horse would go by, this horse would run sideways and be spooky. The rider said that this was nothing new for him, and every time she tried to lope in the past, he would also go sideways instead of loping.

We took a break from the class, and I asked if I could use her horse to demonstrate something. I got on the horse and began walking and trotting around the arena. I asked the other 14 riders to begin trotting, and right when they started, my horse really lost me. He never did anything necessarily dangerous. He was just real inattentive and almost impossible to ride in a semi-straight line down the arena. Every time I would try to trot, he would freeze up or go sideways. It became even more exaggerated as the other horses came trotting near us.

I took this opportunity to explain that the horse wasn't free in his feet, and that was causing all of this spooky-type behavior. When a horse is not relaxed and confident, they cannot move and be "with" the rider in the right kind of way. I placed my hands wide, forward, and low on

WIDE, FORWARD AND LOW

the reins so that when I pulled to turn, I could do it without pulling back on the horse. That messes up their ability to go forward in a natural way. This also made it to where I could be very clear about where I wanted the horse to look, pay attention to, and go.

The second thing I did was completely tune out all the weird stuff that the horse was doing. I focused 100% on what I wanted. I got the horse into a trot and every time he tried to go sideways, I kicked pretty hard so he would go forward. If a horse's feet are moving forward, they will not go sideways. When the horse was thinking of anything besides going, I was kicking. I hung in there, and after a few minutes (and lots of firm, well-timed kicking), the horse was sailing around there at a long trot (and even loping every now and then) as we weaved through all the other riders. He was no longer diving in and jumping

sideways. It was a 180 degree change from what it was before, and it only took about 5 minutes to get it.

In those few minutes, the horse learned several vital things:

1. When I said "get going," I meant it.
2. He needed look where he's going and ignore his surroundings.
3. Going forward and looking straight ahead was very clearly the easiest thing to do.

I also kept about and inch of slack in the reins because I noticed that the rider had constant tension whenever she rode, which definitely contributed to the problem.

With all of this, the horse realized that he had a confidant leader, and that is why he was able to "turn loose", relax, and be a normal horse. As a side note, I did not know this horse and was actually pretty afraid of getting dumped, but I had to pretend I wasn't for the horse's sake. Of course, all of my attention and focus were on riding the horse like a leader, so I didn't have a lot of room left up there for nervousness.

After we were able to trot and lope around the arena for a few minutes, I brought him back down to a walk and dropped the reins. Then I asked everyone else to start trotting again. This time the horse was able to calmly walk along with his head low, on a completely loose rein, and let all the others trot and lope right on by him.

This was night and day different from before when the rider had to constantly hold him back as he pranced around with a high head and

obviously really unsettled.

We go through this same deal with at least 2 or 3 riders at every clinic, and it is always the exact same story. And the same thing has always worked. Remember, the one thing that works on every horse is horsemanship. It more about HOW you do it than WHAT you do.

CHAPTER 21
STORIES FROM COW CAMP
THE SHACK

COW CAMP

This one ranch I worked on was over 1 million acres, and the terrain varied from flat sagebrush, desert, canyons, draws, sand dunes, and mountains that were capped with snow year round. In all of that vastness, it can be expensive and time consuming to get horses and riders up to the east side of the ranch every morning because it was miles from headquarters. Plus the rough terrain made it not only slow going but also hard on trucks and trailers. Because of this, the ranch built several small shack-like structures in these hard to reach places, and they sent a couple of the guys from the crew to live in them and tend the cows in that section of the ranch. These sections include miles and miles of land, and the shacks are called cow camps.

A coworker and I were selected to go to one of these cow camps for the season (around four months). There is no electricity, running water, or cell signal. While at this camp, as long as you get the cows moved where they need to be, you don't have a care in the world, and it gets to be really peaceful. You quickly forget what day it is, and the time doesn't matter. It was perfectly tucked in a small draw in the hills, and the view was amazing. I imagine it was a lot like living in the 1800's.

In the evenings I would rope a dummy and read using a lantern. Many nights after dinner my coworker would just sit and and stare at the wall for sometimes over an hour. I asked him one night what he was

doing. He told me he was visiting his memories. So the next night I stared at the wall with him. It's kind of neat how you find the memories that you didn't even know you had. It all seemed to easily surface when you're staring at a wall only faintly lit by a lantern. Normally, I would never have the patience to do this, but being up there was different because, after awhile, it was like living in a twilight zone or something. It really did seem like time didn't exist.

One evening was different though. I found an old axe in the shrubs behind camp, and the handle was broken, but the blade was still good. So I spent the rest of the evening getting a razor sharp edge on this axe. But we really had no use for the axe blade, so after I spent hours working on it, I just threw it back into the bushes. That's the definition of

being hard up for entertainment.

And then there were the pack rats. They are rodents that like to take shiny or pretty things. It can be coins, pebbles, or any type of small trinket. As long as it has eye appeal, the pack rat will take it if left out on the floor. And they will almost always leave some other small shiny thing in its place. Well, if you're at cow camp, then this a seriously competitive sport. It goes like this... You set something down that you think the pack rat will like and, if he does, he will take your trinket and leave one of his. You literally play a trading game with them. In comparison to our usual nightly routine, this was pretty exciting.

The first two weeks at cow camp the pack rats were too populated in the shack, so we were afraid to leave any of our bedding or belongings in there. They tend to chew holes in them and render your stuff useless. So for the first two weeks we slept outside. I slept in a small tent under a tree next to my cookie stash. One night it stormed really bad and the wind was howling what must have been at least 30 mph. The lightning was hitting all around us. Remember that this camp was 75 miles from any known civilization, had no cell signal, and it took three hours to get a 4WD truck from headquarters up there. We were totally on our own. Sleeping out under a tree (not the best idea) in this ferocious storm made for a long, long night.

The next morning, we went to extreme measures (I will spare you those details) to run the majority of the pack rats out, and we took over the shack.

CHAPTER 22
HANDLING THE FEET

A while back, we got an email and the owner was asking about how to fix a horse that would not let you handle his feet for trimming or shoeing. I had a neighbor who had a horse that was really bad about his feet, so I called him up and said, "Hey, can we come over and use your horse to make a video to show this person how to fix a horse that won't let you handle his feet?" He said, "Sure." A couple of days later we went over there with the camera and he brought the horse out.

The first thing I tried to do was reach down and pick up a foot. I didn't tie the horse up because I knew it was going to move around, and I didn't want it to try and pull back. I held the leadrope in my hand. The second that I started to slide my hand down the front left leg, not to my surprise, the horse started walking off.

It was obvious that I needed to break this down into much smaller steps. So I got a lunge whip and tied a cotton glove to the end of it. Then I started petting the horse with the lunge whip on all four legs, under its belly, etc. I would keep the nose tipped into me a little bit and

let the horse walk circles around me as I was rubbing it with this glove and lunge whip.

After a few minutes of that, the horse got to where I could rub its legs without it thinking that it needed to walk off --- it's obviously hard to trim or shoe if they're thinking 'walk off' every time you try to pick up a foot.

We got that knocked out and then I attempted to pick up the foot and let my hand slide right up to the toe. This would enable me to bend the ankle a little bit which would help me help the horse keep its foot

off the ground. At first, the horse would only let me hold its foot for a few seconds, and then it would either try to walk off, or it would yank its foot out of my hand. This is where the fixing part comes in. Every time the horse said, "Hey, I think I don't want you to handle my feet any more," I said, "Okay, fine." I would give the foot back to the horse and let him have exactly what he thought he wanted. But, there was a catch. That also meant he had to lunge around in circles (do some work).

Now this horse could not really lunge very well, but I could get it to hustle and move its feet around. A lot of what I did was just chasing the hind end while keeping the nose pointed towards me. This would have the horse quickly yield its hind end away from me for about 10 or

12 circles. Then I would allow the horse to stand and catch its breath Then I would pet on it for a few seconds.

After that I would bend down and pick up the foot again. It quickly got to where the horse would let me hold it for 10 seconds or so, but then it got a little bit unsure that letting me hold its foot was the easiest option. I didn't fight the horse or try to keep a hold of the foot. I simply gave the foot back to the horse and then sent him to work again. After about 10 minutes, the horse would stand there and allow me to handle all four feet without much resistance.

There were a couple of times where the horse would let me hold the foot for a pretty good while. Then I would use some good timing and give the foot back before he tried to take it. That was his reward for letting me hold his foot. If he did decide to take his foot back before I gave it to him, we just did the same thing and went to work lunging again.

After a total time of about 20 minutes, the horse would happily stand and let me hold any foot for as long as I wanted. In the beginning,

RELAXED HORSE

the horse thought that it was a better deal for me not to hold his feet. By the end of the session, the horse knew, without a doubt, that it was in his best interest to stand there and allow me to hold his feet. This is one of the best examples of making the right thing easy and the wrong thing difficult. Do not make the horse do it. Set it up and allow him to do it. Let it be his decision. Try to make it his idea to do what you want. I was glad to catch this on film because many horse owners and horses struggle with this issue. My buddy was pretty happy, too, and invited us to come back any time and use one of his horses for a video.

CHAPTER 23
SLOAN'S FILLY

Last summer, a good friend of mine called to tell me about a filly he had recently bought at a horse sale. She was bred really nice, but pretty jumpy on the ground. He could get a halter on her after trying for a little bit, but she stayed skittish and nervous. He informed me that he'd done quite a bit of groundwork trying to get her more gentle, but it didn't really seem to last. He asked if he could bring her over for me to put the first few rides on her. I was glad to do that, but from what he described, I figured he might have to make at least two trips over to my place for me to work with the horse before she'd be ready to get on.

About a week later, he showed up and unloaded the horse. It was exactly like he said. She was extremely skittish. Sometimes, while simply trying to reach and rub her on the head, she would start flying backwards and jumping sideways. I told him we needed to take her over to this large tree stump that I have. The stump is about 3 feet tall and 30 inches in diameter and an important part of my obstacle course. I even carved some steps in one side for easy access. I climbed up on the round stump and had the horse walk circles around me so that she could get

comfortable with giving me her back. When a horse gives you her back, it basically means she gets comfortable enough with a human up above her to where she will put her back right underneath your body. The goal is, with your horse in a halter and lead, to stand on the stump and let her walk around you while at the same time encouraging her to move closer to the stump. Then, when she gets closer, and a little more underneath you, let her rest (reward her). Over time she will become more and more sure about what you're wanting and eventually stand directly underneath you with sureness about it.

What I like about the stump is that you can have the horse continually move forward and go round the stump as you hold the lead while spinning with them as they walk around you. This is convenient in a lot of ways, but mostly because, if they start to go sideways, you can just have them go forward again. We did this for about 10 or 15 minutes, and it got somewhat better.

Then we took a break from the stump and went to the round pen. This was where the real truth came out. If you were a spectator watching this session, you might be thinking at this point that she was beginning to get a little gentle -- that is until you mashed on her a little bit. Mashing is just my word for doing a little bit more than what you're doing at the current moment. In this example, I could be standing next to this horse while moving real slow, smooth, and cautious, and the horse would not react too much. But if I started jumping up and down and moving pretty quickly (mashing), the horse showed me right away that she wasn't okay with that. This is where a lot of people get in trouble.

They assume a horse is gentle and confident with something, but they only expose him to it just a little bit, the tip of the iceberg. But if you can dig down in there, and expose them to the entire iceberg, they may get a little (or a lot) more bothered. When mashing, it's important that you don't get them too bothered, and ensure you stop mashing (release) with good timing. They will very quickly get to where they can handle more and more mashing. So for about 30 minutes, I jumped around and the horse would dart sideways. I just went with her until the feet either slowed down or stopped altogether, and then I would retreat.

After a little bit, I could jump up and lay across the horse's back. There was no saddle on the horse, mind you. I just had a halter and lead rope, and I was holding the lead in my left hand. I would jump up on the horse's back, and she would stand for about two seconds. But then she would jump forward and sideways. She was real uneasy about the whole thing.

After a while of mashing at that level of pressure, I had pushed the line up a good bit. Now I could jump around, even lay across her back for a second, and everything was okay. She wasn't too awfully bothered about that anymore. When she would get bothered, it was really critical that I didn't back off because that would be teaching her that if she got a little scared and jumped sideways, it would all go away. It was critical that I hung in there and didn't retreat until there was a slight change towards her calming down. It didn't have to be a big change, and it wouldn't be, because she was just learning all of this. For example, she would be running sideways, but if she ran sideways a little bit less, I would retreat. If I would have tried to wait until she stood completely still, we would be running around the pen all afternoon, and we would never get anywhere. This is a case of breaking it down to help the horse understand.

Now we had gotten to where I could lay across her back, and she would stand for as long as I wanted, but she had not untracked (moved the feet). Remember, untracking is one of the most important things in training a horse to do anything. Without untracking, you're in a lot of

LOCKED UP

trouble and you may not even know it, until you find that trouble or, more likely, it finds you.

As I was laying across the horse's back on her left side, I shortened up the lead rope, which was in my left hand, and began pulling out to the side being careful not to pull back. I had to pull for about 20 seconds, smooch, and even reach back and slap her on the butt

to get her to begin moving her feet. When she finally did untrack, her foot movement was very sporadic and sticky, not flowy and confident. She would go sideways and then go backwards. After about 20 minutes of doing this, she got to where she could walk forward in a little circle going to the left, and she would do it in a way that looked completely natural. She moved like I wasn't even up there. That's how you know you're getting close -- when you ask the horse to untrack, and the feet move like they would if the horse was just naturally out in the pasture. We'd been at all of this for about two hours, so I told Sloan, "Let's call it good for the day. You can bring her back again next week."

When he brought her back, we had to work on some of the same things again. But this is expected until a horse gets real sure. This time it only took about 10 or 15 minutes to get her back to where she was when I left her a week ago. I explained to Sloan that he would need to repeat doing these things until the horse that he was after (which is the gentle horse that would let me climb all over it and untrack nicely) would be right there on the surface every time. In other words, he would need to do what we had done until he no longer had to repeat it. Before long, that calm, gentle horse would no longer be buried under piles of worry. All of the spookiness and tightness in the feet would just melt away. I put the saddle on her, tightened the cinch (untracking her feet between each tightening) and sent her trotting and loping around both directions in the round pen -- about four times each way. Everything looked good.

She did buck and kick up a little bit, but she wasn't too concerned.

Then, this time with her saddled, I took her over to a panel of the round pen and did some fencing. I basically did the same thing as when I stood on the stump, but I was sitting on top of a panel. After a little bit, because she had already had some of this last week, she got to where she would confidently stand right up underneath me. And now, because I had a rail to help balance, I could put one foot and one hand on the railing of the panel and use my other foot to swing my leg over. She was okay

with my leg being on her back, so I went on and sat down in the saddle. Still holding the fence in case I needed to abort mission, I started petting her all over. Had she gotten real bothered, all I had to do was pull myself to the left a little bit, and I would be right back on the panel instead of on the horse.

We did this for another 25 or 30 minutes to make sure she was real confident. Then everything looked good to go, so I sat on her one more time. This time I put both feet in the stirrups and let go of the panel, all while keeping the halter lead in my free hand.

At this point, you don't want to try and kick a horse to make them go, because they don't even know what kicking means yet. And if you're not careful, it can get them bothered and cause a wreck. A better way is to untrack them by pulling outward on the lead. We did this, and she walked a few steps, so I started petting her. Then we did it again, and I would pet her again. After a few more times of this, I started getting a little more particular. The second that I felt her

getting ready to stop moving her feet, I would start pulling to the left pretty firmly before she even had the chance to freeze up. After five minutes of this, she was freely walking all around the round pen, and did not have any bother at all.

Next I started lightly bumping with my legs in a rhythmic tick-tock type of fashion, increasing the firmness and also slapping my leg and smooching until she would walk just a hair faster. Then once I felt her walk a little bit faster, I would give an instant release and repeated it several times. After this, it was very easy to get her to roll up into a trot because she knew how to escape the pressure (move her feet) that I was putting on her by slapping my leg and bumping with my feet. She rolled right up into a trot and trotted about six steps.

You would not want to ask for more at this time. You would just want to reward that little bit they gave you, and build from there. The second she went up into a trot, I stopped kicking and began petting her on the neck. Almost immediately she came back down to a walk. We repeated this several times, and in the next five minutes or so, I could get her to go right up into a lope, and we loped a few laps around the pen. Then I tossed the lead rope around her head to the other side and we went the other direction.

I stepped off, called it good, and told Sloan that he would probably be fine taking it from there because the whole time he was paying attention and really comprehending what was going on with the horse. But he said he would still like to bring her back for me to ride her in the big arena one time before he took over. A week later he brought her back. This time, it only took about two or three minutes to get that calm, gentle horse that I left a week ago. I started riding her around the arena and letting her go wherever she wanted as long as she went in a forward direction. That's the thing with starting these colts. You don't really want to over-confine them or try to control them too much. Don't focus on that. Focus on getting them freed up, moving out, and going. This is really helpful for preventing much bigger problems later on. The very first thing a horse needs to learn, once you are on their back, is to free up and go.

CHAPTER 24
LUNGING

A while back, a new horse owner asked if I could try to get her horse to lunge because she had tried and tried, but just couldn't get it working. She'd raise the lead rope to try and signal him to move, but the horse would start backing up and turning away instead of lunging in a circle. This is an extremely common problem, but one that's easily fixed. I grabbed a flag and lunge whip, fully extended my right arm outward, and asked him to move by slightly waving the flag in my left hand. And, of course, the horse started backing up instead of turning away from me to start in the circle. While facing the horse, I just went with him while keeping my right arm fully extended outward and using the flag to encourage him to step to his left (my right). This went on for about a minute and a half, and then the horse finally took one step to his left. In other words, he finally, ever so slightly, turned away from me. So I stopped everything, petted him for a few seconds, and then we did it again. This time it only took about 10 seconds, and the horse took a couple of really nice steps towards his left, my right. Remember, we're trying to get the horse to go around us in a circle to my right. Eventually all I had to do was hold out my arm, barely raise the flag, and the horse would simply turn away from me and then stand there.

From that point, all I had to do was keep my right arm (the one holding the lead) up, reach towards his hind end with the flag (in my left hand), wave it a little bit, and he would begin walking forward past me. He would walk forward about six or seven steps and then stop and face me again. This gave me another opportunity to send him back out towards his circle.

After a few times of this, he decided it was easier to stay faced away from me and keep walking forward. Now he was technically lunging around me to the right, but he was at a walk instead of a trot or lope. I let him go a few laps, and I was just real quiet, being sure not to put any pressure on him.

Then I tried a direction change, and it basically fell apart. When the horse went to change directions, he didn't really use his front end and make a nice clean turn. He made a tight half circle and began coming forward right up into my space. I stopped right there and spent a few minutes getting him where I could back him up by shaking the lead rope. Once we got that down, I tried again. But this time, before I asked for the direction change, I had him stop and begin backing. As he was backing, I held up the lead rope in my left hand, and positioned the flag (now in my right hand) to where it would help turn him to his right as he was backing. Then when he turned, he would be moving away from me and not towards me. When he made the turn to the right this time, instead of stepping towards me, I stepped towards him to help his front end

get across the turn. We did this about seven or eight times, and he was finally able to make nice, clean direction changes without crowding me. Within just a few minutes, the horse could lunge to the right, change directions and go to the left, all while staying out at the end of the lead

rope in a uniform circle. The reason that last part of this exercise was so important is because it was teaching the horse to make a direction change without trying to run over the person. It all ties back to the herd leadership dynamic. If the horse is crowding me, and I'm moving my feet away from him, I'm telling him that he is the leader. If I'm inconsistent in groundwork, riding, trailer loading, feeding, or any other area, I'm sending the horse inconsistent messages of, "Sometimes I'm the leader and other times you're the leader." This makes a horse very confused, and a horse cannot follow, trust, have confidence in, or have respect for someone who is always inconsistent. If you have an inconsistent horse, then this is the reason why.

CHAPTER 25
THE SIDEPASS

There was a lady who came to the house and she wanted to learn how to sidepass her horse. So I explained to her that the easiest way to start training a horse to sidepass is by getting the hind end where it is doing most of work. If you can get that happening, then the front end will basically just sidepass all on its own. The reason so many horses don't have a very clean side pass, if any at all, is because one of two things.

1. They are leaking forward too much (walking too forward and not enough sideways).
2. The front end is leading the sidepass.

It's pretty easy to tell if the front end is leading the sidepass because, for example, you'd look down from straight above, with the horse going to the right, and he would be crooked. The front end would be ahead of the hind end. So, getting a really clean side-pass is all about being able to regulate the front end to where it takes a slightly shorter step than the hind end.

After explaining this to the lady, we started off by trying to get the hind end to step left and right, and it took a few minutes. I told her she had to be careful to not have too much back pressure on the reins because this would make the horse feel confined and he may start trying to back up. That wouldn't be good, because in order to sidepass, the horse has have to have a little bit of forward motion. I also warned her not to let the reins become too slack either because then the horse would start walking forward. It's all about finding that balance.

We continued getting the hind end really nice and loosened up. After 10 minutes or so, she got the horse where the hind end was the first part to move when she reached with her leg. Then she was able to move the hind end and have the front end stay in the exact same spot. Being able to slow down or even stop the front end from going sideways while simultaneously moving the hind end is one key to having a nice, clean sidepass.

She was trying to step the hind end to the right, so I told her that bending the neck to the left will do a lot in helping to get the hind end loosened up. But once that gets pretty loose, she would need to start trying to get the same thing to happen with the hind end, only this time, have the neck be straighter with just a very slight tip in the nose -- only a couple of inches. It's really a catch-22 when you start getting the neck more straight. The more bent the neck is, the easier it is to get the hind end to step over, but it can cause the front end to to try to lead the side-pass.

After working with that for another five minutes or so, she was able to step the hind end very easily either direction for several steps all while keeping the neck straight and the front end in the same general

spot. The hard part was done.

So then I suggested to her, "Now, do the same thing you've been doing. Get the hind end stepping around to the right, and as you're doing that, open up the right rein a little bit and that will allow the front end to start leaking to the right. From there, all you have to do is use your

reins to regulate and balance the front end to make sure that it doesn't get ahead of the hind end." She started it up and made a few really nice steps, but then the front end started to lead the hind end. So I asked her, "Do you feel him getting a little crooked? Do you feel that, as you were side passing to the right, the hind end got left behind and the front end was doing all the work?" She said yes, so I explained to her when she feels that beginning to happen, all she needs to do is bring both of her reins a few inches to the left (remember, we are side passing right at this time), and that would slow down the front end.

We took a little break, and when we started back, I suggested that she get the horse side-passing for one or two steps, and then as the horse begins to side-pass, see if she could use her reins and have the front end come to a complete stop, all while having the hind end keep going. She played with this for a few minutes and ended up being able to do it very nicely. Then I asked her to try again and remember to keep that front end in mind and try not to let it get too far ahead. So, she started it up again and got four or five really nice steps that were clean, straight, and even.

I told her to stop right there and just pet on the horse for a minute and let him think about it before starting up again.

We tried again and this time she got six steps. She really could have gotten more, but since the horse was still learning this, I told her it would be a really good idea to release and let him rest for a reward. I said to her, "It's really difficult to do, but try not to get greedy when you are teaching a horse to do something new. They may start to do it a few times and then you think, 'Okay, he's got it,' so it makes you want to go further with it. But if the horse is only half-way certain that he did the right thing, and you keep on asking him to do it over and over too often, he may think, 'Well, gee whiz, I just did a

straight side pass but she kept putting pressure on me. Maybe that's not what she wants. Let me try doing something else.' And then, before you know it, you're back to square one. So it has to be built. Even if they are doing it well, you need to let them know they are doing it well before they start to doubt themselves."

I left her there to work with her horse, and I walked down to the other end of the arena to help somebody else. About 10 minutes later I came back, and she could side pass very nice for about 10 or 15 feet. It was a good day.

CHAPTER 26
THE BUCKING HORSE

This past clinic run we were in New Mexico and there was a fellow who had a really big, dark colored horse. I had been watching how this horse was behaving throughout the groundwork and all of the riding parts of the clinic. The horse was really bothered down inside, but as long as you did things just right, and were very careful, you would not realize that this horse had a lot of bother.

We got to the part of the clinic where everybody practices going from a fast trot to a lope and, while loping pretty fast, this guy's horse started bucking and threw him off. I told everyone that we were going to take a break so I could show them a vitally important thing to learn. Nothing like a buck off to get everyone paying attention and eager to learn!

So, with the owner's permission, I used the bucking horse to demonstrate some essential principles. I walked over and started to rub the horse as I was standing by his side. Nothing really happened. The horse's head was kind of high and his eyes were just a little bit big, but he stood there perfectly still. Then I started jumping just a little bit and rocking the saddle as I was jumping. His eyes got a little bigger and his head a little higher, but he still didn't really do anything. Then I put my toe in the stirrup, jumped a few times, got up and laid halfway across the saddle, and then reached to the other side and started rubbing his ribs with the stirrup on the right side. He stood perfectly still. Then I used my

VERY STIFF NERVOUS HORSE

left hand to pull his nose to the left to try and get him to untrack (move the feet). When that happened, you could really tell how scared of being around humans the horse really was. He didn't move very much. His feet were locked in place. I noticed the same thing during the groundwork portion of the clinic that we did earlier in the day. His feet were really choppy and rough, and the horse's expression made it clear that he was troubled. I could tell just from looking at his eyes that he was unsure and not very confident about anything; the groundwork or the riding.

I suggested that the owner take him over to the mounting block and start trying to get the horse to come up underneath him (like I did in chapter 23). I told him that if the horse decided to step out away from him, to calmly step down and lunge the horse for five minutes or so with lots of direction changes. This would do two things:

1. It would help the horse get better and smoother at the groundwork as long as the rider approached it in a smooth type of way. By doing this, the horse would get more confident and relaxed, which means he would get less spooky on the ground.
2. It would start to show the horse that the best place to be was right underneath the human, because every time the horse did not want to be underneath his owner, the owner would start lunging him and have him work.

He did that for a little while and, about 30 minutes later, I asked to borrow the horse again. I ran him through the same test that I did earlier, and then laid across his back again. This time I mashed on him a little harder. He jumped sideways a few times, and I tried to stay right with him until he got a little smoother, and then I'd back away. After a few minutes of this, everything became really good. He was untracking very smoothly, even with me making all kinds of commotion up there as I was laying halfway across his back.

RELAXED HORSE

At this point, there was a pretty good chance that all systems were go, so I went ahead and swung my other leg over and loped him around the arena five or six times, doing lots of transitions between trot and lope, and everything was fine. Then, when I got off the horse, I looked at his eyes again. He appeared very calm and relaxed. He was licking and chewing and didn't act like a spooky horse anymore. He went through the remainder of the clinic and never bucked again.

A lot of people think that the root of curing a spooky horse like this one is more desensitizing. Desensitizing is a good thing to do, but won't ensure a confident, solid horse. That is why you can ride horses that have been desensitized to everything you could think of, but they are still a nervous wreck when being ridden. At the same time, there are also horses that have had very little desensitizing, like a colt, but even during the first few rides, they are already confident. What makes the difference? Horsemanship.

CHAPTER 27
PAYING ATTENTION

About a year ago a lady called and said that her horse was super inattentive on the ground and under saddle, and it was really the only thing that was hindering her relationship from improving with her horse. So I agreed to meet her at a local arena in my hometown. When she unloaded the horse from the trailer and came over towards me, the first thing I noticed was that she did not have any control of the horse whatsoever. He was basically ignoring her and getting all up into her personal space right from the start. His mind was on everything but his human. I said to her, "If a horse does not know that he is supposed to maintain some space from you, unless you ask him to come in close, then he will also not be able to pay attention to you because, in order for him to not crowd you, he has to be paying attention to where you're at, when you stop, et cetera." I explained that the way she will be able to fix this horse's inattentiveness is, "Just get him better at his ground work -- get him where he's not crowding; get him where he can lunge without coming in and running you over."

So the first thing we did is the first thing we do at all of the clinics. I had her stand out in front of the horse and begin shaking the lead rope until the horse took a step back. At first she started to wiggle it just a little bit and the horse immediately started to walk forward. So I

yelled, "Shake it big, shake it big; shake it as hard and as big as you can! Shake it, shake it! Watch his feet, watch his feet!" But then the horse started going sideways, and then he went forward again. I had her hang in there until the horse finally took a step back. "Freeze, right there," I said. So she completely quit moving the lead rope the second the horse took a step back. I told her to walk up and rub the horse on the head, but watch very closely and if he starts to walk forward, begin shaking as much as needed to get the horse to take a step back. So after about 10 minutes we got this working to where the thing that was happening last was now happening first.

So then I told her, "Okay, now you've got a little control. Try leading the horse around this arena and see if you can keep him at least

six or seven feet behind you." At this point the horse had already started being more attentive because she gave the horse a reason to be attentive. And I told her as she was walking, "If the horse starts to gain ground

or get closer to you, just plant your feet and start shaking the lead and put him back at the distance that he's supposed to be. Then you can simply turn and continue walking again." After about three laps she had the horse where he would stay back at the very end of the lead, six or seven feet behind her. So then I told her, "Okay, now as you're walking, glance over your shoulder and look right at the horse's feet. As you do that, I want you to freeze in your tracks. When you do that, the horse should freeze in his tracks, too. He should stop instantly. If he doesn't, begin shaking the lead and show him that he was supposed to stop. And

it would probably be a good idea to back him up a couple steps just for good measure." So the first time she tried, the horse did get stopped before he got to crowding her too bad, but he didn't freeze in his tracks. So I told her to keep working. About 15 minutes later, when she froze the horse froze. It looked really good.

At this point, the horse was much more attentive to her because, if he wanted to avoid having pressure put on him, he would have to pay attention to her. So by now you're probably seeing how respecting personal space and other groundwork will fix inattentiveness. It all goes hand in hand. A horse can not have nice groundwork and ignore the human at the same time. It's impossible.

Then I told her, "Okay, now that you've got him pretty good at knowing about respecting your space and keeping a distance from you,

I want you to try lunging him at a walk and see if you can get him to go around you and do a few direction changes -- but keep the horse out on the circle. Keep him out away from you." I handed her a flag and explained that she could use it as a means to an end. The flag would save her a lot of energy, and also help her be much more clear with the horse. I said, "If he is getting close, be certain that you do not move your feet in a way that is yielding to him because that will be one of those small things that, later on, will add up to inattentiveness, spookiness, et cetera." I told her, "If anything, if he does start to crowd you, I want you to move towards him and be pretty dramatic about it. Really wave your arms and really wave that flag and smooch at him. Do whatever it takes to get his feet to yield to yours, not the other way around."

After a few minutes of this, she could very nicely lunge her horse both directions. And then I said, "Okay, let's go over here to the corner of the arena where we first started. I want you to face me with your back to the horse, and we're gonna have a conversation about the weather. But at the same time I want you to keep an eye on your horse. If he starts to

BLA, BLA, BLABLA, BLA

look away from you, or drop his head to sniff the ground, or do anything but look right at you, I want you to stomp your foot and put a quick shake in the lead rope. We practiced this for a few minutes and now the horse would not take his eyes off of his owner. It looked really good. It was a 180 degree change from when she first came into the arena.

Now I told her that she was ready to get on. The groundwork was good, and as long as she could be consistent with what she had learned, in no time she would not have to watch the horse so carefully. He would be in habit of paying attention. You know how people say that when it comes to a horse, habits are the easiest thing to make and the hardest thing to break? Usually when they say that, they're referring to bad habits, but the same holds true with good habits.

She mounted her horse and I instructed her to begin walking around the arena. The horse started getting inattentive again. So I instructed her to slide her hands down her reins to where there was only a couple inches of slack in each rein. I said to her, "Keep your hands really wide, forward, and low. And that way if the horse goes to look to

WIDE FORWARD AND LOW

the right, with only an inch or two of slack in that left rein he will immediately run into that left rein. Make sure you keep your arms pretty stiff and rigid so when he does find the end of your rein, it will not be a mushy feel. It will feel to him like you really mean it. It will feel to him like you are serious that you want him to look where he is going, not at his surroundings."

She worked on this for about 10 minutes, and then I instructed her to try to ride with one hand and see what it looked like. Everything looked great and the horse was no longer looking around. I said to her, "From this point, if he does look around, it'll only be real slight, and you won't have to use 30 pounds of pressure to get his attention back to center so that he's looking where he's going." I told her that now she could probably just use her legs to direct his attention back to the center. 'Center' is the center of his body. So if the horse is

looking to the left, you would need to wiggle your right leg a little bit, and that will pull his attention back to center. She worked on this for a little while. I told her to try some of her normal maneuvers such as trotting circles, backing up, side passing. It all looked really good. She told me that the horse had never done it that lightly before and everything felt great.

So see, as simple as it is, just getting a horse in the habit of paying attention to the rider will very easily improve everything else. But you have to remember, if you cannot give your horse a reason to pay attention to you, it is unfair of the rider to expect the horse to pay attention. Be ready and willing to give the horse a reason.

CHAPTER 28
CROSSING OBJECTS

Now that you're familiar with untracking, I want to try and help you connect the dots of how it ties into everything else. Untracking the feet does a lot to help with trailer loading and crossing obstacles, of course, but the main thing untracking the feet does is free up the mind. A horse's mind and his feet are directly connected. This story is about a horse that someone sent quite a few years back. This was one that needed a lot of help untracking, and it was the most difficult one I've ever had that I can remember.

DIRECTLY LINKED

He was a little black-and-white paint horse that had about 20 rides. I started this horse for the owner, and it was coming along right on track. I had already worked on getting his feet freed up as I do with any horse. It's actually one of the first and most important things to do with

a colt. If you've ever noticed when trying to lead a horse, if their feet freeze up and they stop going forward, if you will just walk off to the side, and then pull their head over a little bit, it will untrack them, and they can continue walking forward again. That is how you get them to take their first steps under saddle with a human on their back. Horses don't just automatically know this stuff. It's up to us to teach them.

After riding this paint horse out in the woods a few times, and needing to cross a small creek on the trail, I realized that we would need to do some extra work on confidence crossing objects. When we got back to the house after a ride, I took the horse over to a pallet that I had picked up from town. I had also stopped in at a farm store and grabbed a black rubber mat that was about an inch thick and the size of the pallet. I laid a sheet of plywood over top of the pallet and underneath the black mat just to help reinforce the strength of the pallet.

So with my obstacle set up, I jumped on the horse and walked him up to the pallet. I tried to get him to step up on the pallet using just very slight leg pressure and, of course, nothing happened. The horse tried to dodge the pallet and go around to the left or right. While we're on this part, it's also worth mentioning that this exercise really helps a

horse learn to stay in between your reins and legs, meaning they will develop a pretty confident sureness about not leaning on your leg or your rein.

When the horse would try to go around to the left of the pallet, I would stop him and bring the front end back to the right where we were centered with the pallet again. You have to understand that when a horse thinks they cannot cross an object, they really do think they cannot cross

it. Adding too much leg or other type of coercion just builds up more and more pressure until you get the champagne bottle syndrome --- if you shake and shake it, before long the top will blow off. You don't want the top to blow off, especially on a horse. Usually the more you pressure them into going across the object, the more they will try to evade and the busier you have to get to keep them from evading.

What works much better is to get the horse as close as they will get to the object, and that is what I did with this horse. I rode him up to the pallet as close as possible, and then I slid my hand down my right rein and pulled out to the side, being sure to pull directly out, trying very hard to make sure I did not pull back in any way. Once I did that, the front end took one step to the right, and then I slid my left hand down the left rein and put slack in the right rein. From there I did the same thing again, but only this time on the left side. I pulled directly outward to the left and the horse's head bent to the left but the feet did not come. I just hung in there holding the head with that left bend and, after waiting about 10 seconds, I then started pulling a little more. Still, the feet did not come.

So I started pulling a little bit more with a pumping action. I would smoothly pull 10 pounds, and then a quick release, and then smoothly pull 10 pounds again, and then another quick release. That got the feet unlocked. After that the feet took one step to the left, so then I switched back and did the same thing to the right, and so on. After about three minutes of this, constantly keeping the front end going left and right, left and right, left and right, the horse took a little bit of a step forward as the front end was going left and right. If you pay attention you can feel when this happens. I felt it happen so I instantly released the reins and petted the horse for a few seconds. Then I started it up again.

The more I did this, the more the feet were figuring out, "Hey, if I just let my foot leak forward a little bit the pulling will stop." That's exactly what happened. After another few minutes, the horse tried to drop its head to inspect the pallet, so I was sure to really feed out

the reins with a lot of slack so the horse could freely drop its head to examine -- also being ready to gather the reins back up in case the horse tried to walk around the pallet instead of over it. After allowing the horse to examine the pallet for a few seconds, I then pulled the head back up and started untracking the front end again. Total allotted time at this point was probably 8 or 10 minutes.

Then a foot went forward and I heard it bump the pallet. That deserved a few more seconds of full release. I gathered back up and started again. This time the foot not only bumped the pallet, but the horse started pawing the pallette. That's always a good sign. It means they are beginning to think about it.

After a couple more minutes, maybe not even that long, both front feet were up on the pallet, and I was standing there with loose

reins rubbing the horse on the neck. Then we started it back up again. Left, right, left, right, left, right. Pulling until the front end would begin to loosen up and move just a little bit. By then the horse was as far forward as it could go without putting a back foot up on the pallet, so we repeated again. Left, then right. Left, then right. Then a back foot came, and at this point the horse quickly jumped all the way over the pallet. So we started again.

The horse did cross the pallet after a total time of about 15 minutes, but it was still pretty rough and choppy -- more like a jump. He really rushed it, so we walked back around and repeated again, except for this time it only took about two minutes to get the horse to go over the pallet. Then we came around again, and it only took about a minute before the horse jumped the pallet, but he didn't rush it quite as much.

I thought to myself, "Hey, maybe I should just try to stop the horse once it gets up on the pallet". But then I thought, "No, if I just keep going it will smooth out. That would be the better thing to do here."

We went around about five more times and, at this point, the horse was calmly walking right over the pallet like it was not even there. Now I would be okay to try to stop the horse and see if I could get him to stand on the pallet.

You see, I didn't want to try to stop the horse and get in the his way when he tried to cross the pallet until he was certain that crossing the pallet was an easy and simple thing to do. Now I felt that the horse was pretty sure and confident about it.

It was a pretty small pallet, and I had to time it pretty accurately, but after a couple tries I was able to get the horse to stop and stand on the pallet. Then I tried to see if I could get him to back off of the pallet because I knew I would be trying to teach the horse to trailer load in the next couple of days and this would help tremendously. We practiced that for a little bit and it all cleaned up real nicely.

When I had previously worked on getting the horse to cross the creek on the trail, I did the same thing I did with the pallet, and the horse did cross the creek, but it was rough and choppy. But this time, now that the pallet work had been done, we came to the creek and it only took about 10 seconds of untracking, pulling left and right, to get the horse to go right across the creek and this time it was smooth. There was no rush and the horse did not attempt to jump across it.

I wanted to test and see if the horse really was sure enough about crossing these objects to where it would be just as good even if I gave it a few days off. For the next few days, I just did some arena work --- backing, stopping, etc. Then a few days later, we went back to the creek in the woods, and it was the exact same result. The horse smoothly crossed the creek after only about 10 seconds of untracking.

That is another thing to remember here. Just because a horse does something one time does not mean they are sure about it. They have to do it several times before they even begin to get slightly confident about it. Some horses get confident real quick, but with the average horse, it'll take more than one time before they are certain that they can or can't do these different things we try to teach them. Always be willing to hang in there and reassure your horse if they get a little bit unsure.

Some people reading this may be thinking, "Yeah, but I do that. We've tried to cross the same creek a hundred times and it's always the same." But you have to remember, it's not what you do, it's how you do what you do. Try approaching it a different way. If the training you are doing is not seeming to stick with your horse, then something needs to change. When it begins to stick, you will know you're getting warmer with the approach.

CHAPTER 29
STORIES FROM COW CAMP
THE ROCK CHUCK

One time there was a rock chuck. If you don't know what a rock chuck is, it's probably pretty closely related to a beaver. Just think of it as a giant squirrel. Anyway, we'll get to that in a little bit. Some years back, I was working for this ranch, and I had come down from cow camp for the weekend. I was going to town to spend my paycheck on more fancy bits and whatnot. When I got in my truck, I noticed a slightly stinky odor, but it was pretty faint. I had to go back in the bunk house because I forgot my wallet, and I mentioned the smell to the guys, but no one was too interested. They were all watching some movie about a cartoon lion and a crazy monkey that, oddly, reminded me of Wayne.

ROCKCHUCK

So I looked around in my truck for a few minutes thinking it was just some old food or something that was causing the smell. I couldn't find anything, so I jumped in and went to town, ran my errands, and got back to headquarters the next night. I saddled up my horse and trotted back up into the mountains to cow camp and didn't think anything more about the stinky smell in my truck.

The next week when I came back out of the mountains, I got in my truck, and the smell was much worse. So I started sniffing around and noticed that the stench got really strong the lower my nose got to the floor of my truck. I finally located it. It was under the driver's seat of my pickup. It was some type of dead animal.

I ran inside and told everybody that there was a giant, dead squirrel underneath the seat of my truck. This time they were a little more interested. Everybody ran out and we were all wondering how it could have happened. Henry said, "Did you leave your windows down? I wonder if it crawled in there sometime during the week and then thought it couldn't get back out and just died or something." And then we all went through different theories of how this rock chuck could have crawled up into my truck and died. Well then I noticed that Wayne was being pretty quiet, which seemed oddly suspicious. So I said, "What do you think happened, Wayne?" He kind of put his head down, trying his hardest not to make eye contact, and came up with some lame theory.

But he wasn't very good at hiding his guilt because the whole time he was saying what he thought could have happened, he was about to explode with laughter.

It was pretty clear at this point. We all decided that Wayne was the culprit, and he had placed the dead rock chuck in my truck. And then, of course, everybody started busting out laughing. I tried not to join in, but I couldn't help it. It was pretty hilarious even though it did take about a week before the smell finally subsided. This is where it gets good.

I figured I couldn't let that slide because I lived with Wayne up at cow camp, and if I let him get away with that one, the pranks would surely continue. So I had to wait until pretty late when everybody was inside or off doing something else. I think Wayne knew I was planning some retaliation because when I tried to place the same dead rock chuck in his truck, the doors were locked. But Wayne's truck was really old, and it had a sliding back glass with a busted latch. He didn't think about that.

I had to shimmy through the back windshield, but I was able to get the rock chuck underneath Wayne's back seat. I figured I would put it there because it would be harder for him to find. I timed it just right to where soon after I did that, we had to head back up into the mountains for cow camp for another week. This way it would be 5 or 6 long days for the smell of the rock chuck to get all inside of Wayne's pickup. My prank was going to be way better than his because was my truck sat in the shade for the week, and Wayne's was going to be sitting in the sun.

Another week went by and nothing happened. I expected Wayne to come hunt me down at some point after the next weekend, but he never did. Well, I always came down from camp earlier than he would to go to town on the weekends. But come to find out, Wayne did not even use his truck that next weekend. It just sat there in the sun all weekend and then, of course, that weekend was over so we had to go back up to cow camp for another whole week. I was growing really impatient because I wanted to see Wayne's reaction and how awesome it would be. But then I decided, in the long run, it would be worth it because in my truck the rock chuck was only under the seat for a week in the shade. But Wayne's truck ….. oh, yeah. It was gonna be way, way, way worse. I reasoned that the extra week would give the rock chuck even more time to rot away under the seat of Wayne's truck. And it did just that. So finally, we came back down the next weekend and I tried to discreetly ask Wayne if he was going to town. He said he was because he had to deposit his paycheck. Wayne didn't really like going into town. At this point I started getting real excited. Just like always, I had gotten down from camp a few hours before him. I chose to ride my horses down from camp because it saved about an hour. Wayne chose to come down in the pickup even though it took about three and a half hours to drive back down to headquarters.

I had taken a shower and gotten dressed and was getting ready to go. As I walked out of the bunkhouse, Wayne and all of the guys were standing in a circle around the front of his truck with that rock chuck laying there on the ground. Everybody was laughing except for Wayne. He wasn't super mad. After all, he couldn't be. But he was trying really

hard to act like he was. He picked the dead carcass up by the tail and then came at me, running as fast as he could. He was a older guy, maybe in his late 50s, but he was in really, really good shape. I thought I would be able to outrun him, but I couldn't. I couldn't outrun him at all. My excuse is that Wayne was from that area so he was used to the higher elevation and lack of oxygen, where I wasn't. That's the story I'm sticking to.

After about 15 seconds of running, he tackled me and then held me down and started literally beating me with that dead rock chuck. I was screaming like a girl and laughing by now, and Wayne and everyone else was just rolling on the ground. It was quite a scene.

There are a couple of things I wonder about when I think of this story. One thing I wonder is if, even to this day, the smell of that rock chuck is still in Wayne's truck. The second thing I wonder about is actually something I just now thought of as I was telling this story. During the time I worked on this ranch, I took a few days off and flew back to Florida for a visit. When it was time to catch the plane, I did like always --- trotted my horse down from cow camp back to headquarters. But I was so excited for the trip, that I skipped taking another shower or putting on clean clothes and just jumped in my truck and headed to the airport. I figured people were staring at me because I was dressed a la buckaroo and had dirt on my face but, looking back, I can't actually recall if the time I was beaten with the dead rock chuck was the same week that I trotted out of cow camp straight to the airplane to go to Florida. Now I think maybe they were looking at me because I still smelled like a dead rock chuck.

CHAPTER 30
THE HORSE THAT DIDN'T WANT TO BE CAUGHT

There was a horse that had a reputation for being difficult to catch, so we used him as an example horse to make a video on catching. A hard to catch horse can be a major frustration, especially when you're on a time schedule. We got to the facility where the horse was being kept, and there were several other horses in the paddock with this brown horse. It was not a real small paddock, but not a huge one either. Maybe about half the size of your average rodeo arena. I walked in and all the horses were standing still, pretty much together. I approached the brown horse that was hard to catch in such a way that would push him out and away from the other horses, and give me a chance to get him sorted out -- similar to the way it's done in a cutting horse competition where the rider will position his horse to cause the cow he has selected to leave the herd.

After doing that, I was able to single out the one I wanted to catch. This brown horse was on the south end of the paddock, and all of the other ones were behind me. I had to be careful to stay midways down the paddock. I didn't want to be in the north side really deep with

THE HARD TO CATCH HORSE

all the other horses, and I also didn't want to be too far into the south end because if I did that, then the pressure of my presence would cause the horse to pop out of the south end of the paddock and very easily run right by me. As long as I kept a little distance from the horse, I would have a chance to work a line left and right to try and keep the horse contained in the south end of the paddock until it decided to stand still and stop trying to run by me to get with the other horses.

It did come trotting right towards me pretty quick after I got him separated, but it was not because he was trotting to me; it was because he was trying to get past me to get to the other horses. I was able to block the horse and have him stay on his side of the paddock, which was the south end, but if he had gotten by me and mixed in with the other horses, I would've simply just sorted them out again. After a bit, the horse would realize that no matter how many times he ran by and got with the other horses, he always got sorted back out.

Once I blocked him a couple of times, he would happily stand there, but he wasn't looking at me. From that point I just stood still, staring right at him, and after about five or six seconds, the horse bent his neck a little bit to look my way. I instantly turned around and walked off about 10 feet. I wanted to be sure to give the horse a release when it did what I wanted.

Then the horse started to come towards me, yet again, to try to get around me, but I was able to use this to my advantage and have the horse stop where it was, parallel to the fence on the south side of the paddock. There were a couple more times when the horse started to move around and all I had to do was basically work the east/west line again. When I say work the line, I mean like how a goalie would go back and forth across the goal in soccer to continually block the ball from coming into the goal. I was the goalie and the horse was the ball. All I had to do was hold my line.

By this time the horse had gotten pretty settled and was okay with the idea of just hanging out --- no longer trying to run past me to get to the other horses. That would've been an excellent time to quit for the day. But since we had a limited amount of time to work with this horse, I decided to keep working at it.

From there I slowly started walking towards the horse, and every time the horse looked at me, I would turn around and walk off. I did that for three or four minutes and got the horse really confident about looking at me. If a horse is shown that the path of least resistance is to look at what is trying to catch him, he will be much easier to catch. In order for a horse to turn away and not be caught, they have to stop looking at you. Training a horse to look at you when you approach them is a handy thing to have.

I continued to build on this until the horse got pretty sure about it, and then I gradually started getting closer and closer. Now, even if the horse was looking at me, I would go on and step a couple steps closer and then, instead of turning around and walking off, I would just turn around and stand still. I waited for a few seconds and would turn back around and begin walking towards the horse. When it looked at me, I would stop and turn around, but not walk further away. Again, I turned and walked towards the horse until it looked at me.

At this point I was about three feet away when the horse turned and looked at me. This time I stopped walking towards the horse but did not turn around. The horse looked back straight again. I was off to the horse's right just slightly. So I took another half a step closer and stood and waited, looking at the horse. This time when it turned and looked,

VERY POSITIVE CHANGE

I took half a step back. Then I did it again, except this next time when I took half a step back, the horse's front end stepped one step to the right, which was a really good positive change --- remember that I am to the horse's right side so when the front end stepped one step to the right, that meant the horse was drawing his body a little closer to me. Since that was such a big change, I once again turned around and walked off about 10 feet. One reason I did that was to reward that change and another reason I did it is because I wanted to do all of this again to get the horse even more sure about it.

I repeated all of the above, and then the next time I was about three feet away, and the horse turned and started to look at me, I instantly backed up a few steps. The horse started to follow me. I turned around and walked about five or six feet up the fence and then stopped and turned around to face the horse. He was right behind me.

From there, I reached out and starting rubbing the horse on the forehead, and then as I was doing that, over a period of 30 or 40 seconds, I gradually worked my way around to the side of the horse's neck. This whole time I had the halter and lead in my hand, so I took just the end of the lead and put it in the hand that was rubbing the horse's neck.

From there, I gradually scratched the neck up towards the mane and then worked the end of the lead down over the top of the neck. Now I could reach under and grab the other end of the lead and have the horse pretty much caught.

This is a good technique because if the horse does try to leave, you can step back and pull on the looped lead rope which will help them stay put and turn them back towards you. From there, I slid the halter on and voila -- the horse was caught.

Everything we did was not actually about catching the horse --- what we were trying to do was get the horse ready to be caught. If it would've been my horse, I probably would've spent the next four or five days doing these little sessions, and maybe even have a handful of grain to give the horse when it would turn and look at me, or any time he needed a reward. While we're on this, a lot of people wonder, 'Is it okay to give horses treats or grain from your hand?' Once again, this all depends. Some people say that this will make a horse pushy on the ground and that is very true, but what if you were to have the horse move away from you and only gave him the treat or the grain from your hand once he was consistently staying at least five or six feet away from you all on his own? Then you would step towards the horse and give him the grain. That would actually teach a horse to be less pushy. This is just one example of how everything depends on everything else. A video showing this session is on the membership site: http://members. carsonjames.com

CHAPTER 31
NECK REINING

One time a guy sent a horse for me to ride and he said, "The only thing that I want this horse to be super good at is neck reining, so make that a top priority." The horse was only going to be with me for 30 days, and it's pretty unorthodox to try and ride a horse on a neck rein that only has 30 rides. But since that was so important to the owner, I figured it was worth a shot.

I started the colt in a rope halter, as I usually do. But this time, I was going to see if it would even be possible to get a horse to neck rein on the very first few rides. I did the untracking and we loped a few laps around the pen and all the usual stuff. I didn't really even try to steer him. I just got him to moving around a little bit. But then I started picking up the halter lead and tried to have him go to the right with the lead being on the left side of his neck and vice versa. It looked about like you think it would. I tightened up the lead and pushed it on the left side his neck, opened up my right leg, closed my left leg, and not much happened at all. His nose tipped a little bit to the left and, since we were neck reining, I would hope that it would tip a little bit to the right. But I have also hoped for a million dollars and didn't get that either.

Anyways, the nose went to the left, but I was able to immediately apply a little bit more pressure on the lead so that when his nose did go to the left, it ran into more pressure. I was also ready to give him a little slack for when he tried to take his nose back to the right. Or, at least take

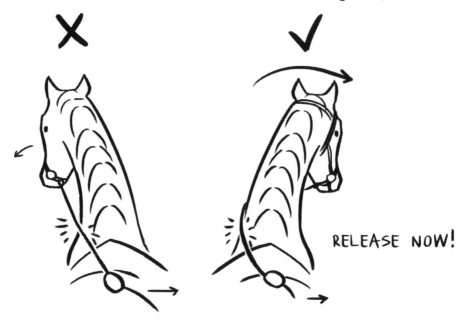

it a little bit less left. After five or six seconds, it was not very much, but he did attempt to straighten his neck back out just a hair, so I gave him a completely slack rein and petted him. I worked this for about 10 or 15 minutes and, at this point, I could pick up and press the lead on the left side of his neck, and his nose would tip slightly to the right, and then his front end would also take a step to the right.

The next day, I rode him in an arena and all we did was walk or either stand still, but I was constantly just throwing the lead back and forth from the left side to the right side, tightening it, trying to get his nose to tip the correct direction for being able to neck rein. Every now and then, even if his nose was in the correct direction, I would still hold it until I felt him actually turn that way just a hair. We worked on this for a good hour and a half at a walk, and by the end of the session, he could walk circles and figure eights off of nothing but a neck rein. It was only his fourth or fifth ride.

We continued doing this throughout his 30 days. I never once rode him two-handed. It was always on a neck rein. Sometimes it was a little awkward because I would have to force myself to just hang on him and wait for the nose to tip the correct direction and/or the feet to go the direction that I wanted before I would release. But as long as you're paying attention, you would be amazed at how quick it can happen. I would now say that a colt can learn to neck rein just as quick and easily as he can ride two-handed. It's just that it requires more paying attention and more feel and timing.

That's something interesting about neck reining. Ideally, when you neck rein the horse to the right, you want his nose to tip to the right. But technically, if his nose tips to the right, he is pushing against pressure, and you always hear that a horse should yield to pressure. But when neck reining, that is really not the case. You actually want their nose to push into that neck rein. A way to reword it is, imagine sitting on your horse with both reins even. And then you put both reins in the same hand and you begin to bring your hand to the right. Well, as you're bringing your hand to the right, you are actually tightening the left rein, and as that rein continues to tighten, at some point, it is going to pull the horse's nose to the left. But in this situation, you are trying to get the horse to turn to the right, therefore, his nose should tip to the right. Neck reining is more about operating a horse off of a feel instead of just a basic pressure and release. If a horse was strictly yielding to pressure, when we squeeze with our legs, he would jump straight up off the ground. Just something to think about.

CHAPTER 32
THE MULE

Some years ago, this lady sent me a mule. She thought that it would be really funny, and a good experiment, for me to try to put a barrel pattern on this mule. She was actually wanting to try and barrel race on it. But the mule had really, really bad feet. Like, really, really bad. So the first couple of weeks, I didn't even ride the mule. I just trimmed its feet, and did some groundwork. Then, I was able to get several rides on her, and it wasn't too bad. I could trot circles and figure eights. The mule actually had a pretty smooth lope. I had loped her out in the woods and down some trails, but she was still pretty green.

Then I noticed that the mule had a crack in its hoof wall, so I did the best I could to get that fixed, and gave her another few weeks off. I told the owner that the mule might have to be there for quite a long time to get 30 rides, just because of the feet. She agreed. I think I actually ended up having this mule for three or four months before I got 30 rides on it. The point is that the mule had quite a bit of time off and had not been ridden much.

There was a little jackpot barrel race in a town just south of where my barn was at the time. The owner called to say that she was going to be there with her horses entered in the barrel race, and asked if I wanted to bring the mule and take it slowly through the pattern, just to see how it would do. A few weeks earlier, I had actually taken the mule around the barrels several times, so I knew she could trot around the barrels, and maybe even lope a couple of strides in between the barrels. So I told her, "Yea, what the heck. It would probably be entertaining, and people would enjoy watching it."

I loaded up the trailer, and got down there with the mule. Because she was still very green, and had not been ridden in a few weeks, I lunged her around for a few minutes. Everything seemed good, so I stepped on and rode right off without a problem. I noticed that she had gotten really heavy to my legs, but I made the mistake of not getting on the mule until just before time to go in the arena, so there was no time to work on that.

We trotted around the barrels, and everything went well. After I rounded the third barrel headed back towards the alleyway, I thought, "Okay, now this is a good time to kick her on up into a lope. It would

be even more funny if this mule was loping." I had to kick pretty hard once again, but she did start to lope. At this point, it was just a big yee-haw moment, and pretty funny to watch. I had taken off my hat, and was swinging it around in the air, and people were hollering. The entertainment goal had been achieved, so I thought. Then I got a little bit too excited, and got greedy. I did something that I definitely should not have done. About halfway down the arena I thought to myself, "Man, it would be neat if I could get the mule to run pretty fast. That would be even more funny." She was already loping pretty decent and, for her, that was dang impressive. But me, being excited, started kicking more to try to get the mule to run faster. As I was swinging my hat around in the air and not paying attention, she suddenly planted her front feet, and did this little buck/rear up type thing. I was already leaning forward pretty good on a loose rein trying to get her to go faster.

Exactly what you think happened, did happen, but it was actually a little funnier than that. I came off the mule and did a full entire front flip in the air, and somehow managed to land directly on my feet standing right in front of the mule. I turned around and looked at this mule, and she was just standing there staring at me. She didn't continue to buck or run off. She was perfectly placed only a few feet from my landing spot. Then I realized that maybe everyone thought that was all part of the show. So I took a bow, and everyone started clapping. They may have thought it was entertaining, but I knew what really happened --- I had been outsmarted by a mule.

CHAPTER 33
LAYING DOWN

There was a stock contractor, the guy that brings all of the animals for rodeos, that I knew fairly well because back in the day I used to work for him, and he was a close family friend. I got a call from him to say he had a horse that was just kind of, sort of broke. You could ride him but he didn't really have any handle on him. He was wondering if I would take the horse for 30 days and try to tune him up and also get him easier to be caught.

When I picked the horse up, the guy mentioned that he was getting older, and this was already a pretty big horse, so he wanted me to be sure I got the horse really good at standing still to be mounted. I told him I do that anyway, but I would spend extra time on it just to make sure it's really, really good.

After I put several rides on the horse, I got this amazingly great idea. I thought to myself -- how funny would it be if I could teach the horse to lay down to be mounted and get him so good at it that it could be easily done. If I could pull it off, when I took the horse back to the stock contractor, I could show him (implying that he was so old he couldn't step up in the stirrup) and we could get a few laughs. I also knew that I would be returning the horse to him at one of his rodeos, so I knew that when I was showing him what the horse could do, there would be other people around to see which would make it even funnier.

Now, I had never taught a horse to lay down to be mounted before, but I assumed that it would be the same basic principle as everything else. Reward the slightest try and the smallest change, only ask for little pieces, and only ask for more once the little piece seemed consistently good. So every time I would ride the horse, I would spend about five minutes getting the horse closer and closer to laying down.

I did this by putting a rope around his front left foot and running it up to the saddle horn. Then I would pull the foot off the ground, take a few wraps around the horn, and pull back on the reins until he started to shift his weight rearward and lower his front end. When that happened, I would give him an instant release. Then we would pick up and do it again.

This went on for the next three or four rides for about five minutes of work every time I rode him. After a week, I could pretty much lay the horse down very easily. At this point, I was giving him a handful of grain every time he would go all the way down. Once he would get all the way down laying on his side, I knew that I would also have him stay down with no tension on the reins or help from me. So I started having the reins slack and leaving it completely up to him. If he started to get up, as long as I was quick enough, I could use the reins to catch him and help him stay down on the ground.

The first couple times, I was only wanting him to stay down on his own for 10 seconds or so. The more we worked on this, the better he got at staying down all on his own. Near the end of the 30 days, he was so good at it that you no longer needed the rope on the foot. All you had to do was stand next to his rib cage just like you were about to get on him, use your toe and rub his foot, and he would pick it up and hold

it off of the ground. At the same time, you would also apply a small amount of back pressure to the reins. He would slowly and smoothly go down into a bowing position and then he would collapse his hind end, and be laying on his side. Not completely flat, but like a dog would if he was cooling off in the shade. I was always sure to give him a little

grain and lots of petting when he would stay down on his own. He got to where he really liked laying down. Why wouldn't he? It was a super awesome deal, and every time he got down on the ground, there was absolutely no pressure being put on him.

From there, all I had to do was swing my leg over to sit on him. Then I could just hold on the saddle horn and push with one leg to rock him a little bit and up he would go. I was really excited to have this where he would do much of it on his own just before time to take him back to the stock contractor.

I hauled him up to the rodeo, and when we got to the arena I unloaded the horse and saddled him up. Then I told the owner, "Now, this one has a special trick. I've never done it for any other horse, but I did it just for you because I know it may help you out." Just like we had practiced, I rubbed his front left foot with my toe, the leg came up, and at the same time I pulled back on the reins just a little bit. Down he went smoothly and easily, and he was completely content to stay down as long as there was nothing pushing him to get up. So I swung my leg over and then pushed off with one leg to rock him and, up he goes. It was a big hit.

I guess the moral of this story is that even if you're doing something you're unfamiliar with, or have never done before with a horse, though it is true that every horse is different, remember that every horse thinks and operates the same way. Once you understand this, trying to teach one something new can be pretty easy.

A couple of months later, I was at another rodeo visiting with one of the guys that worked for the stock contractor. One of his jobs was to saddle all of the horses, including the one I had taught to lay down. He told me that this horse used to turn away from the person trying to catch him and pin his ears. He said, "You had to watch him because he had kicked at people a couple of times." He also told me that the horse always seemed to despise people in general. But then he said, "Now, after getting the horse back, he no longer turns away, doesn't try to kick at people anymore, and just seems a whole lot happier." The point is that I was not even aware the horse had these bad little spots, but this just proves again that everything is interconnected. This is just one example.

CHAPTER 34
BACKING THE HIND END

There was a clinic last year where a lady had a horse that got really sticky in his feet. No matter how hard she pulled, it would not back up. Usually, this is the first sign of becoming a horse that rears if something doesn't change. This horse was not thinking about rearing yet; he was just completely frozen in his feet.

By now you understand untracking and how great it is, and this is how you can use untracking to fix a problem like this. The horse was feeling the oncoming pressure, but he just did not know how to handle it. She started off pulling with just a couple pounds of pressure, and then, when nothing happened, she pulled a little harder. Then she was maybe at five pounds or so. Still nothing happened.

At this point, with the horse's lack of understanding, not knowing how to release through his feet, if she were to put any more pressure on him, it would bind him down more and more and more. It would be like these two walls were closing in around you. All you had to do was jump out from in between the walls to escape the pressure, but you did not know that you had the ability to jump out of there.

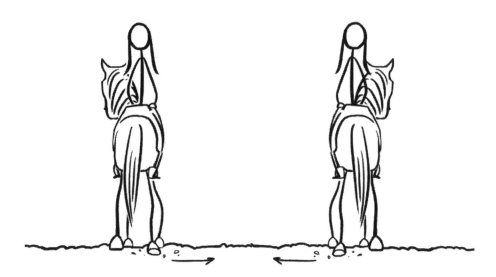

In this situation, I told the owner to start getting the hind end moving left and right. It's actually the same thing you do when trying to get the front end turned loose to cross an object, except you work on the hind end instead. It's all about getting the horse to turn loose in his feet. When a horse backs up, you ideally want them to pull themselves back with their hind feet instead of push themselves back with their front feet. If you can get their hind feet moving left and right a little bit, and then, as the feet are moving, begin drawing with some back pressure on the reins, this will cause one of the hind feet to reach back as it is going left or right. Looking over your shoulder helps a lot to know when to release and pet for a few seconds. Right when you see that hind foot reach back some, you immediately switch over and push the hind end the other way. As you are pushing it, let's say, to the right, you look over your left shoulder down at that left hind foot. As the hind end is stepping laterally to the right, you begin adding back pressure and watch that left hind foot. You will notice that as you add the back pressure at some point as it is moving across there, it will come off the ground and go more back than over. That

SWITCH!

is the timing for the release.

Then you switch and do it on the other side. After she repeated this for about four or five minutes, the horse got to where she would pick up a light feel on the reins and the hind feet would immediately turn loose. She was just connecting the hind feet to the pull on the reins. It's similar to a bicycle or a car. You can't really direct it if it's not moving in the first place. For some horses, you have to break it down a little bit more than just pulling when they're not backing and releasing when they are. For some horses, you have to first get the hind feet moving. Directing where they go comes a little later. With these new skills, after a few more sessions of work, the horse was backing nicely and lightly. Changing her approach made all the difference.

CHAPTER 35
CROSSING OVER

This story is really the same old movie, but it happens so often that I figured it was worth putting in here. You may or may not have seen a person who is struggling to get the front feet or hind feet to cross over. But, it's a very simple thing to get a horse to do, and probably one of the easiest, once you can steer him a little bit. It's all about getting the balance just right.

When I say the balance, I mean just enough leg, just enough rein, just enough back pressure, but not too much; making sure that one hand is in the right spot and making sure the other hand is in a good spot also. It's like trying to balance a broom up in the air on the tip of your finger. If you can get the feel and timing pretty close, the broom will really balance on its own, even though the only thing touching it is the tip of your finger.

We'll start with the front end first. There was a friend of mine who told me that she had been trying for a few months to get this horse to walk in a tight circle, and then make the circle tighter and tighter until it turned into a little spin. The horse was doing it very nicely except when he got tight in the turn, he would suck back a little bit and try to back up as he was turning. This was preventing the front feet from crossing over. Let's say the horse was going to enter a spin to the right. You want the front left foot to come off the ground and go forward a little bit, but at the same time it would need to reach way to the right in order to cross over in front of the right front foot. It all has to do with forward motion. The reason this horse was not able to cross over in the front end was a lack of forward motion.

I suggested that she try to not have any back pressure on the reins and just keeping thinking forward, forward, forward. This time when she started to wind down into the tight circles I told her, "Don't think about the spin or getting him to cross over. Just open up the right side of your body (and his), and then keep riding him forward and to the right, forward and to the right." After a couple of tries, the horse crossed over beautifully and she took a break for a few minutes. Then we talked about what had just happened.

CROSSED OVER

After about 10 minutes more work, she could come right into the spin and the horse could go round and round and cross over every step. She still had to watch and be ready to kick him forward if he tried to suck back through the turn, but she did well with that. She had to catch him to prevent that from happening a few different times, but her timing was good and the horse quickly learned what she was wanting him to do. The back feet are the same. The reason a horse can't cross over in the hind end is same reason that a horse would not be able to cross over in the front end. He does not have enough forward motion.

I invite you to stand on the ground. Right now, where you're at, stand up. We're going to try and get your left foot and right foot to

DON'T LEAN
FORWARD!

operate like the hind end of a horse. Your left foot would be the horse's left hind foot. Your right foot would be the horse's right hind foot. You're not allowed to take a single step forward. You're not allowed to even lean forward. I'm about to ask you to move your hind end one step to your right, but I want you to cross over, meaning I want your left foot to cross over in front of your right foot when it lands. But remember, I've got a brick wall right in front of your toes. You're not allowed to reach forward with that left foot. If you follow these rules, you will notice that it's impossible for you to cross over without the ability to go forward because your left foot runs into your right foot. If you got really tricky, you could pick up your left foot, move it back a little bit, shift your weight to the left foot, then you could step your right foot over. Doing this, you could move to the right, but you would have to move your left foot back to do it, and it would not cross over in front of the right foot. It would not be until I took the brick wall down and said, "Okay, walk forward, but very slowly. Take real small steps. I want you to leak forward just a little bit. As you are slowly taking these small steps forward, when your left foot comes off the ground, bring it and cross over your right foot." You will then notice you can very easily cross over and stay in nice balance. You also don't have to worry about hitting yourself in the right foot with your left foot. You will also notice you don't get tangled up and everything becomes easy.

Again, it's all about the approach. Anytime you want a horse to cross over in either end, just let him have a little bit more forwardness, but make sure he is going to the right or left at the same time, and voila.

CHAPTER 36
BAND-AID

Before I tell this story, I want to first say that anytime you have to cross a downed barbed wire fence, be sure to hit that sucker at a long trot. Don't do it at a walk, whatever you do. Or better yet, just don't do it at all.

This little incident happened when I was working on a ranch in Arizona, just south of the southern rims of the Grand Canyon. It was great scenery, but the horses had been handled pretty rough up until about a year before I arrived at the ranch. There were some new people running this place, and they were more into horsemanship than the last group of people that ran it previously. These horses were pretty ranch-y, which means they were hard to catch, hard to saddle, and the first 10 minutes of every morning, you'd better be alert because if you weren't, you would probably end up getting bucked off. But after trotting about 10 minutes, they were so gentle you could put a kid on them and they would be fine all day. This is your typical ranch horse.

This particular day, I was on one of those ranch-y horses. His name was Band-Aid (that should have been my first clue). When they

assigned Band-Aid to my string, they told me that the reason they called
the horse Band-Aid is because every person who had ever ridden him
ended up in the hospital. But they said the horse was a lot better now,
although no one had been on him in a year, so it was a pretty sketchy
situation. But I had to be a tough cowboy and, of course, I did not let
anyone know that I was scared out of my mind to get on this horse. We
actually went for 10 or so rides over the first couple months that I was
there, and I never had a problem. But he always felt like one of those
ticking time bombs. Every time you started to do something, you never
knew if it was going to set him off. I should have found the time to work
with him some to try and get him better, but it was a busy time of year,
and we were working daylight to dark.

Crossing an old, barbed wire fence is something that I would
never do unless I absolutely had to, but these guys would cross right
over them and not even think twice about it. I had done it several times
lately, so I was getting a little more used to the idea of it, but still not
crazy about it.

We were out gathering some cows on a big plain that had about
a 10% downgrade and a somewhat rocky terrain. There were some cows
on the other side of an old, downed fence and they were in the section
that I was supposed to gather. I had no choice but to go get them. I had
still not crossed any downed fences on Band-Aid -- it had always been
on other horses that I trusted a little more than him. So I thought the

smart thing to do would be to try and cross it at an extremely slow walk and watch his feet. I thought to myself, "Okay, if I'm really on my game, I can strictly control his feet, right where they land, and we can get across this fence without either one of us dying."

But the first step onto the fence, Band-Aid stepped on a piece of fencing that was run through a staple in an old post that was about five feet away. I realized this when I heard that awful squelching noise that happens when a fence gets pulled really hard across a post. Then I felt the horse kick with one of his front feet. That was when I realized something bad was about to happen.

The horse shot backwards and sideways, both at the same time, in a jump type shuffle, and the only thing I can figure is that a little bit of the barbed wire got caught between the heel of his shoe and the heel of his hoof because, as he flew back, a couple strands of barb wire and half of that fence came with us. It was already a super scary situation, but then the horse turned and bolted down the hill, back towards where the horse trailer was parked. He bolted for a few steps, and it was all happening so fast that I couldn't look around, but it felt like the barbed wire had come loose.

Turns out that it did but, after running full out for those first

couple of steps, he put his head down and started bucking pretty hard while running down this hill. I really was not ready for it. I was still trying to figure out if the wire had come loose, so I was pretty slow to respond -- not that I could have ridden him out if I had been alert. I'm just not that great of a bronc rider.

I lost my right stirrup and it's all pretty blurry at this point, but I ended up slipping off the right side of the horse and my left foot was caught in the stirrup. I didn't get drug for a long way -- I figured maybe 20 feet or so -- but I do remember that my left leg was hanging across his rump, just behind the cantle of my saddle, and I could feel the air of his hooves grazing right past my head. His back feet were that close. It's really a miracle that my head didn't get kicked or trampled.

My foot finally came out of the stirrup and I was free from the horse, but during the wreck something happened to my knee. I couldn't stand up. I just laid there, slightly propped up, watching the horse run the mile back down to the trailer. You could see where the trailer was parked from where I was. It was pretty open country.

Then, I just laid my head down and reminisced about how happy I was to be alive, and the only thing messed up was my knee. After a few minutes, I looked up again to see what the horse was doing, and I noticed one of the guys chasing him around in big circles. He eventually

got him roped and then they tied him up to the horse trailer and started riding towards me.

I took off my chaps and started waving them to try to signal one of the guys that was out looking for me. Then the pain got really bad, so I just laid back down and closed my eyes. About five minutes later, I heard the sound of a horse's hooves grinding across the rocks. I looked up and saw one of the guys, but he rode right by me. He didn't even see me. I was laying in some sagebrush hidden from view. I was able to call out to him, and then he made a left turn and came over and found me. He stayed with me until they could unhook the truck and get it up to where I was.

The cow boss took me to the nearest town, which was about an hour away from ranch headquarters. They took an X-ray and then gave me a shot, but by the time we actually got to the hospital, I could already bend my knee a little bit and could even walk on it with a limp. They put me on light duty so that I didn't have to rope or brand, so I got a chair and spent the rest of the day reloading the vaccination guns for the guys that were giving the calves shots after they got drug in to be branded.

I iced my knee all night and was back riding the next day. It still bothered me for a while and you'll even see a knee brace in some of our videos. I eventually did get to where I trusted the horse named Band-Aid more. I was finally able to spend a little time doing some fencing and other things I would do with a colt (back to the basics), and he got a lot better. It didn't feel like he was a ticking time bomb anymore, but I still never did take that horse, or any other, over any downed barbed wire. I may always have a bad phobia about doing that.

CHAPTER 37
DEWEY CASH

Ironically enough, this event that I'm about to tell you took place about two weeks before the incident with Band-Aid. This was on a different horse. It was a really stout, good-looking horse named Dewey. He was solid black and reminded me of Johnny Cash, so I started calling him Dewey Cash because he was fully dressed in black.

We were in the branding pen, and this was my first time branding off of Dewey Cash. The cow boss informed me that the guys who had ridden him in the past were all right-handed, so I would need to gradually introduce roping to him because I am a left-handed roper and everything is on the opposite side of what this horse is normally used to. The cow boss was really good like that. He never did push anybody to do anything they weren't comfortable with. He was probably one of my favorite bosses.

So I rode Dewey Cash into the herd of cows and calves and made a really small loop. I did not even try swinging it for the first 30 or 40 seconds. I just rocked it a little bit. He seemed okay with that, so I made a slightly bigger loop and then rocked it a little more. Then I made a normal size loop and gave it one swing and quit. You can see where this is going.

After about five minutes I could swing the rope on his left side and he wouldn't get bothered. There's a lesson in that, too -- gradually expose the horse to something new, and do it only a little bit at a time. The trick is to know when the horse starts to draw the line. You push up until the point where you're about an inch below that line, then you hold right there until you feel the horse allowing that line to fade. That's when you immediately stop whatever it is you're doing that was bothering him. If you can get the timing on this right, you can very quickly get a horse used to just about anything, even if he seems completely terrified of it. It's all in the timing. For some horses, just simply doing it over and over will not cut it. They need a more gradual introduction.

Anyway, back to the story. Dewey Cash was now to the point where I could swing the rope on him and all was well, so I rode up behind one of the calves that had not been branded yet, and I didn't really even try to rope it. I threw the rope and just let it hit the back legs of the calf to see how the horse would respond. He seemed fine with that, so then I figured he was good enough and we could go on. Now I know what you're thinking. The horse is about to come unglued when I start to drag the calf out to be branded. But that isn't what happened. He handled me roping the hind feet of the calf. He handled dallying the rope around the saddle horn. He even did well turning the opposite direction than he normally does. With a right handed roper, the horse would turn left and head out of the herd of cattle up towards the branding fire and the vaccination crew. But he had to turn the opposite direction because I'm a lefty, and he did it with no problem. Then, after walking about 30 steps, the calf was almost to the branding fire, so I started to let a little bit of rope slide to allow the horse some freedom of movement to get turned around to face the calf. Since the rope was on the left side of the horse, I needed him to turn left. When I was just about ready to turn him

left to face the calf, Dewey Cash took over and quickly turned to the right. I did have my reins offset so that my left rein was a little bit tighter than my right rein thinking I could get a little hold of his nose if he tried to turn right, but he turned real quick, and I just didn't have enough rein to catch him. This caused the rope to wrap around his butt and go under his tail, and then it's pretty much all history from there.

 He took off back into the herd of cows for about three jumps bucking. By the third jump he had me pretty much hanging down by his shoulder. I was still more or less on his back, but awkwardly balancing on his withers. I looked like a trick rider. My head was about even with where his right leg attaches to his shoulder, and my belly and my ribs were right up against his front right side.

 The horse started spinning which tangled and wrapped the rope around me so that I was now tied to the horse --- which is never a good thing in any circumstance, unless you're one of those monkeys that rides the dog to pen sheep during a rodeo act.

I was attempting to get my dallies popped loose as I was still hanging off the side, but Dewey Cash was turning in the opposite direction that he would need to be turning for a left-handed roper. I was suspended in midair, but still tied to the horse for just a jump or

two, and then enough rope finally slid around the horn to free me from its seemingly magical grip. It allowed me to land and hit the ground. I actually didn't get hurt this day. It was a good day.

In the weeks leading up to this event, if time had allowed, I could have roped a log and pulled it around to get Dewey Cash more in the habit of turning the correct direction for a left handed roper. That probably would have kept that wreck from ever happening.

If you miss out on preparation, something unexpected may happen and you will think, "Well gee, that's weird for him to all of a sudden do that," but he's just been holding back the whole time, and you've just been lucky. I'll take advantage of this story to stress to you the importance of preparing your horse ahead of time for the things you are about to do. Don't for one second allow your mind to make yourself think that your horse has got this good enough. Usually, the statements go like this -- "Yeah, I mean, he was still a little bit spooky, and he doesn't like to lope. Last time we tried that, he bucked me off. But he does everything else so wonderful, and he is just so gentle on the ground. He's a big teddy bear, always in your pocket. It doesn't make sense why he would do that." But once you've studied horses for a little while, it makes perfect sense. For example, the fact that the horse is always in your pocket shows that the horse does not think or realize that you are supposed to be the one in control. Therefore, the respect and the confidence have no possible way of being there. If I had to count them,

I would say there's been at least 200 times that a clinic participant would walk up to me leading their horse and then begin telling me about all of these things that their horse does that they would rather him not do. They don't even realize this, but as I am standing there listening to them telling me about the problems they're having with

their horse, their horse is directly behind them doing the very thing, one of the key things, that causes all of the problems they are telling me about. The moral of this story is be aware, be aware, be aware. Remember Dewey Cash.

CHAPTER 38
THE BOLTING BAY

When I was 17 years old, and still pretty green, I worked for a performance horse trainer starting colts. They were really well-bred colts, and the trainer I was working for was a good hand with horses. He was one of those trainers who could get the horse's body and feet to do just about anything, but the horse was always in a bothered frame of mind while doing it. They were able to fill in because they had a lot of confidence on the horse's back and were definitely strong leaders, but they sure didn't mind jerking on one's mouth pretty hard if he didn't do something exactly right. For reasons like this, there would be times the colts would get a little hot and bothered, especially if trotted out through the pasture away from the barn and then turned around to head back. They were light enough in the mouth, so you could definitely slow them back down, but the fact that you had to constantly re-slow them is a red flag that there are still some pieces missing.

The trainer was really big on heavy lateral pulling during the first 10 rides or so to get them bridle-wise. I won't go into a lot of detail about that, but it's basically where you slide your hand down a rein as

low as it can go as you are trotting, and then you sit down and pull that rein back and out to the side about as hard as you can. Before the horses know about this, they will just freeze up with a really bent neck and not move their feet. But after having this done several times, just sliding your hand down and lifting the rein would cause the front end to step over real nice and free. I have veered away from doing this over the years because there's not a lot of pre-signal going to the horse before the heavy pulling starts. In my mind, that's not fair to the horse.

So this day, I was on one of my colts, and it was about the fourth ride. They told me to slide my hand down and pull her around a little bit both ways. I had done this before, but not to the degree or the amount of firmness that they were telling me to do it now. So I slid my hand down and pulled pretty hard. The horse locked up her feet a little bit, so the trainer said to pull harder with a pumping motion. I was pulling about as hard as I could and then finally the horse did move its feet, but not in the way we were hoping for. She grabbed the bit, straightened her neck, and took off bolting. I was in the arena so I really wasn't that worried about

it. I was able to tip the nose and bend the neck a little bit and, after about 30 or 40 seconds, I managed to get from a dead run down to a fast trot. I kept working it down slower and slower from there. But that incident had some repercussions.

For the rest of the time that I worked there, every time I would get on this particular bay horse and try to turn to the right, the horse would bolt. She had gotten to where she was really stiff and hard in the neck and in the mouth, so pulling the head around was pretty near impossible and, at a fast speed, I really didn't want to do that anyway and risk flipping my horse over on top of me.

My plan was to do some fencing with her and just an extra day or two of groundwork because she was still pretty fidgety, even when being saddled and mounted. But that's the way the head trainer wanted them so they would be able to, in their minds, keep them really light and responsive. This went on for the next few rides, and then the trainer told me that I needed to take this horse out in the hills and ride her outside of the arena because this would help the horse, in their words, get over 'being stupid'.

A few days later, much to my dismay, I went out into the hills and started trotting the horse out away from the barn. I noticed her tip her nose a little to the right and when she saw me out of her right eye, that eye got really big. I thought, "Oh no," and sure enough, away she goes with me on board. It was over some pretty rough, rocky, and steep hills. Remember that I was only 17 at the time, and I was just learning about horses, so I didn't really know any better. But even to this day, I would not want to get on that horse out in an open pasture the way that she was at that time. I had a job to do, and I didn't really have a choice because I was there for the summer. It wasn't like I could just pick up and leave because I didn't even have a vehicle. I would wake up with cold sweats and shaking because I honestly thought that every morning was going to be the last day of my life. That may have been a little bit dramatic of me, but there were a few different occasions where the horse bolted and headed right towards a cliff, and it really seemed like she would have run right off the edge if I could not pull hard enough to get her turned. It wasn't a good situation at all. I decided then and there to become the type of horseman that could take a horse like this one and know how to 'fix' the issues that were causing her to be so lost that all she knew to do was run away.

Looking back on it now, a little more fencing and just getting the horse more okay with people in general would have made a big difference. It still took several minutes to get her caught, and you had to do it just right if you even stood a chance. You still had to hobble her to get a saddle on, so some more sacking out and untracking definitely would have been beneficial. When you're working with your horse on the 'little' things, always remember that it's the 'little' things that turn into 'big' things. Take the time to fill in the 'holes'. In the long run, you'll be very glad you did.

CHAPTER 39
THE TIGHT COLT

This is a story about the 'magic' of getting a horse to trot really fast. A friend of mine brought over a colt that he had started. It had about two weeks worth of riding. Now you could kind of steer it around some, but the horse felt really tight and bothered. It never really felt like it wanted to buck, but it felt like at any moment it could start wanting to. The horse also felt like it was always moving crooked. Even when you were going in a straight line, you would have sworn that there was something medically wrong with the horse. He assured me the colt was sound.

I had a tarp hanging down from a board that is suspended high in the air in my pasture as part of my obstacle course, so I thought, "Well, I'll go over there and use this to try to build some confidence and communication." I would point the horse at the tarp and walk up to it. It was flailing in the wind, so I could only get within about 15 feet of it at first. After untracking the front end, left and right for two or three minutes, I was now five feet away from the blowing tarp. I continued this, and before long the horse would get really close to it. After the whole allotted time of about 15 minutes, I could walk the horse back and

forth through the tarp.

Then I rode right over to the huge, round stump that I also have in my pasture and did some fencing. I spent a little time getting him to where he would get right underneath me as I stood on the stump. After doing these two things alone, he had a complete change in his facial expression. His eye got really soft and relaxed, and then when I stepped back on him to ride around some more, his head hung naturally like it would if he was out in the pasture trotting or walking around. That's how I knew that it was getting better.

I still had a pretty hard time getting him to go up into a trot. He still felt bunched up, tight in his feet, and pretty awkward. But I also knew that the trainer had a tendency to ride with contact pretty much all the time, so my theory was that this was the reason why the horse moved so awkwardly. It could also be the reason the horse was still skittish-acting even though it already had two weeks of riding.

From there I just ignored all of his awkwardness and started trotting the horse around in random directions out in the pasture. Every now and then I would ride a little bit faster to see if I could gradually work him up into a longer trot. Basically, I was trying to wean

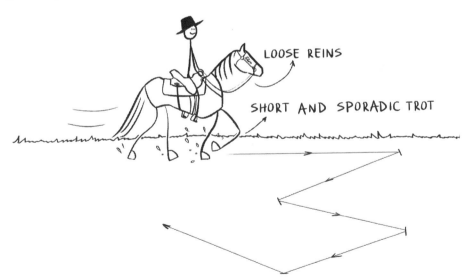

LOOSE REINS

SHORT AND SPORADIC TROT

him into extending his trot. It took about 20 minutes or so, but the horse finally started to turn loose enough, mentally and physically, to trot out real nice and free on a loose rein. I'm pretty sure that's the first time this colt had ever been ridden on a loose rein. It was a horse that I did not

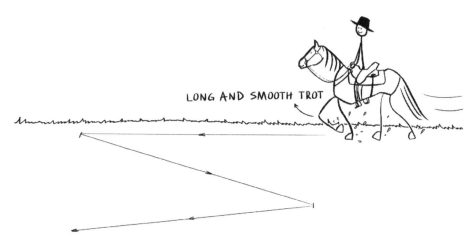

LONG AND SMOOTH TROT

know, and I could tell he was still unsure about some things, so I only put about an inch of slack in the reins, kept my hands forward wide and low, and kept a deep seat with my legs slightly out in front of me -- just in case.

The horse was also somewhat inattentive, so keeping my hands real nice and wide would help me begin getting him in the habit of looking where he was going. This clarity is part of what attributed to the horse getting more and more relaxed as we trotted around. I have found that, in the horse's perspective, trotting really fast and loping are really similar in their mind. Of course, if the horse is running away with you at the trot gait, and always gaining speed without you asking him to, then that's a whole other story. If this is the case, then you would want to get that part worked out first.

But assuming a horse is normal, and only goes as fast as you ride them, this is one of the best things you can do for a horse -- and what I did for this colt. Get on their back and hit a long trot. Keep your hands forward wide and low. Focus on helping the horse look directly where he is going. Be sure you've got a couple of inches of slack in the reins so you're not hanging on the horse in any way. That will start making them jumpy. But, with only an inch or two of slack, you will be quickly ready to help them if they need help.

So after I got him okay with the tarp and did some fencing, we could trot all around that pasture without me having to hang on him. He was looking where he was going. He was now calm and confident, but not lazy. It was feeling really good.

Then I tried to extend the trot even a little more hoping he would roll up into a lope, and he did just that. He loped a few strides, but still felt tight. Then I picked up and tipped his nose to slow him back down. I noticed that his downward transitions were really rough. For the next 10 minutes I would roll him up into a lope, and then get in his way by

tipping the nose and let him find the downward transition. I did not try to make him slow down. I just fixed it up and let him find it. After about 10 or 15 of these, he felt much more balanced -- not only when he was slowing down, but also when he was trotting and loping.

By the end of the session the colt was a completely different horse. He felt much more balanced, and he was definitely way more relaxed and confident. His eye was soft and I could even move around him on the ground pretty briskly and he would not get spooked, whereas before we did all of this, you had to be really careful saddling him and moving around him on the ground. Otherwise, you would be picking your saddle up out of the dirt. Once again, this is just another story of how some of the most basic things can cause the biggest difference. It probably only took about 45 minutes to get the colt from being very tense and unsure to being a perfectly normal colt that was fine with being ridden around. He and I both seemed to feel very good about the whole situation.

CHAPTER 40
THINGS TO DO WITH YOUNG HORSES

This happens pretty often, but I'll narrow it down to one instance because I basically tell everyone the same thing on this subject. As usual, during a clinic last year, someone came up and said something along the lines of, "Hey Carson, I've got this colt. He's just now turning two but he's still pretty small, and I'm a pretty heavy rider, so I don't want to start him quite yet." I congratulated them on making that decision. They proceeded to ask me, "What are some things I can do with this colt to get him prepared for being ridden." I told them all of the usual things --- he needs to be good at respecting your space; make sure you can lead the horse and the horse is not leading you. In other words, make sure the horse can be led around and stay back away from you. Make sure that when you stop walking, the horse freezes in his tracks immediately. Make sure you can back the horse by wiggling the lead rope. It's not a bad idea to rope the feet and teach the horse to relax and yield his legs when they are pulled on by a rope.

And all of this would help a whole lot in the long run, but I explained to them that there's two sides to the story -- we'll talk more

about that in a minute. One of the other suggestions I made is to find
a situation where they can put some horses together and use a flag to
move them around an arena, or a round pen, or a pasture. I told them
how to get the horses where they really no longer wanted to run around
in a group. I said, "Just make sure that when they are running in a group
you keep the heat on. Try to position yourself where you will have a
chance to separate them. When they separate even the tiniest bit, take the

pressure away. Rinse and repeat. Before long, if you were to cause three
of the six horses to lope out through the pasture away from you, the
other three horses would not take off to catch up. The three you didn't

push out to the pasture would not feel compelled to follow the others. It doesn't take that long, and you really can get horses to where they are like this. It can go a long way towards stopping buddy sour before it ever starts. This is just one of the things you can do on the ground to get a horse where they really don't have any desire to be with other horses when there is a human around.

Another suggestion I made was an idea I got at one of the facilities in Salt Lake City, Utah where we did a clinic. It was a brilliant setup. The owners of the arena had some long ropes hanging down from

the rafters of the arena. They would tie up a younger horse to the rope, and then they would turn a few other horses loose in the arena and run them around with a flag. At first, of course, the young horse tied to the rope would run circles around the rope and get all bothered. But after about a week of it, he would not even pick his head up, but would stand there with his leg cocked, even if there were 10 other horses running around in the arena. If I had rafters above my arena I would definitely do this. I think it would be very beneficial.

Now, here's the other side of the story. I went on to say, "As far as buddy sour goes (and this is an extremely common issue), there are some things you can do to help stop buddy sour, or barn sour, or trailer sour, or whatever -- but wouldn't it be better to never even have to deal with the 'problem' at all? The reason a horse would get really buddy sour while being ridden is because the horse felt like he could not get his security and comfort from his rider. Therefore, he had to seek it by other means. For example, bolting back to the barn, always wanting to be next to other horses, or even rushing to get back to the trailer. The other side of the story is, you need to work diligently to increase your horsemanship, your leadership and your communication. The better all of those things get, the more confidence and trust the horse will have in you. Therefore, he will not need to always have a buddy because, as corny as this sounds, in his mind his buddy is right there with him."

Ironically, after I had just spent 10 minutes explaining all this to one person, another person came up and stated that their horse always freaks out when the other horses leave because that means he is all by himself. So I told them that they were exactly right in their evaluation of the 'problem', but what they would have to learn to do is convince the horse that he was not really by himself, even though all the other horses were gone. Yes, you can do exercises to cure buddy sour, but you don't really want to have to depend on that if you can just get yourself to where the horse looks to you like he would the herd leader. Then he would be mostly buddy sour to you.

CHAPTER 41
THE CROOKED HORSE

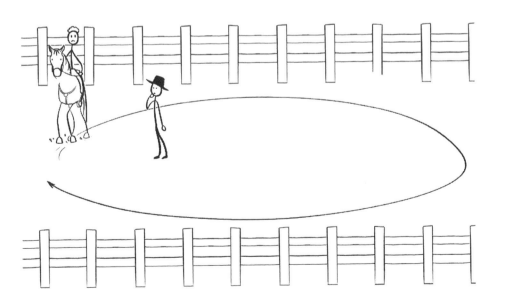

Once you start to understand some horsemanship concepts, or maybe not even fully understand them, but you know enough to be aware that things can happen in one part of the horse's body which cause other things to happen at the other end, this can help you greatly in terms of fixing crookedness in a horse.

Once I was helping a lady who had a horse that she wanted to back up straighter. He backed pretty nice and light, and really did not look that heavy as I was standing on the ground watching. But the horse would definitely back crooked. If she backed the horse for 20 seconds, she would end up making a 30 foot circle in the arena. It wasn't just slightly crooked. It was really crooked. When she would try to back the horse, the horse would also turn a little bit to the right as he was backing. This caused him to back giant circles.

I asked her to think about what was happening. I said, "Okay, tell me what has to happen in a horse's feet in order for him to turn right as he is backing." She thought for a second and said, "Well, the front end would have to turn and reach out a little bit to the right as he was backing." I told her that was exactly right, and I added that the

horse is probably also stepping to the left with his hind end, and this is contributing to the crookedness. So we worked on both ends, but where it really ended up shining was when we worked on the hind end.

I told her to try and back a few steps as I stood right in front of her. The second that I saw the horse's hip move to the left (it was easy to see when it would happen because I was standing directly in front of the horse), I said, "There, did you feel it?" She told me that she felt it, so that was great. Being able to feel it happen, or able to feel it getting ready to happen, is the hardest part.

So then I said to her, "Don't worry about trying to fix it. Just spend a few minutes backing up and say, 'Yes', right when you feel the hip pop out. We need to make sure that you can consistently feel when the hip is straight and when it is crooked."

After practicing for a few minutes, she'd gotten to where she could nail it spot on every time. So then I told her, "This time, start backing your horse up and be ready to tip his nose." She was familiar with controlling the hind end, and she already knew that whichever way the nose tips, the hind end will pretty easily go the opposite direction of the nose. It's pretty difficult for the hind end to go the same direction as the nose. I told her it would not take much and to be sure that she doesn't get so focused on tipping the nose that the horse stops backing.

I told her to mainly focus on keeping him backing, and when she feels the hip come out, to just very slightly tip the nose to the left. Remember, the hip is going to the left, which is causing the horse to back crooked. So she tried it for the first time and was ready to tip the nose the instant she felt the hip drifting to the left and she also nailed that spot on. She picked up a little more tension in the left rein causing the nose to tip to the left. I told her, "That's perfect. Now, just maintain that and keep him backing."

After three more steps, I saw the hip come back straight again. In other words, the hip stepped a little bit more to the right, back where it was before she started backing. I said, "Drop the reins right there and pet him."

I asked her if she felt when it got 'right' and she said that she did. So then we did this for about five more minutes and released every time the hip came back to the center. She was now able to back five or six steps before having to tip the nose. I told her to continue doing this, but don't try to back straight for too long. I told her that, in the ideal situation, she would release the horse and let it stand before he got crooked. Then, each time, you would try to get him to back a little further and a little further without getting crooked. But now that she could tip the nose, she would be able to get him straight again before releasing and letting him stand. This way, he would not continue backing more and more crooked.

We took a break from that and I told her to work on the front end. Remember, the front end had a tendency to drift to the right a little bit as she was backing, causing the horse to back a big clockwise circle.

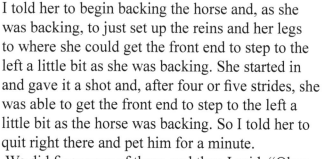

I told her to begin backing the horse and, as she was backing, to just set up the reins and her legs to where she could get the front end to step to the left a little bit as she was backing. She started in and gave it a shot and, after four or five strides, she was able to get the front end to step to the left a little bit as the horse was backing. So I told her to quit right there and pet him for a minute.

We did five more of those and then I said, "Okay, forget everything we just did. Pick up the reins and just back him like normal," and he backed a perfectly straight line for about 15 feet.

Ironically, the very next day, there was a clinic participant with a horse whose hip would go to the right every time they tried to stop him which caused him to stop crooked. So I got on that horse for a few minutes and stopped him from a walk and a trot, but as I came down with my reins to stop the horse, I would pull the right rein a little bit more causing the nose to tip to the right during the stop. That made it very difficult for the hind end to come to the right. Therefore, the horse's feet would be straight. Then, right after stopping, I would step the hind end another step to the left to counteract or counterbalance what would normally take place. After

about 20 or 25 practice sessions, the counterbalancing caught up and the horse was able to make nice, straight, balanced stops.

You can also use this when trying to open a gate. Let's say you ride up next to a gate, you're getting ready to open it, and the horse steps his hind end to the left away from the gate. Well, if you can just be ready to tip the nose slightly to the left, you can use that to allow the hind end to run into a wall when it tries to step away from the gate. Tipping the nose to regulate the hind end can also be used in flying lead changes, side passing, and many other maneuvers. Look at it as a means to an end. The goal is that you should not have to tip the horse's nose in order to get the feet to be straight and balanced, but it's definitely a good tool to have in your arsenal to help the horse until it becomes natural for him, and he no longer needs his nose tipped to find it.

CHAPTER 42
AUNT JACKIE

This story actually involves a relative of mine. She had two horses. She said that when her husband would lead one horse to turn it out into the pasture after being fed in the mornings, she would follow behind with the other horse. The only problem was when they would go through the gate into the larger pasture, her horse would bolt right through the gate and usually snatch the lead rope out of her hands, take off running, and then they would have to re-catch the horse just to remove the halter. The other horse that her husband led through the gate would not do this. He could simply go through the gate, remove the halter, and release the horse.

So I thought this would be a really good time to get video footage on how to fix this issue. We went to her place and set up the camera and the microphones and all that good stuff. Then I had her describe to me what the horses were doing. I said, "Okay, first let me see you lead the horse around and make sure that the horse can stay a good distance behind you. Make sure that when you stop walking, the horse instantly freezes in its tracks, and make sure that you can get the horse to back up pretty good by wiggling the rope." The horse had done some of this before, so it had the general idea of all the things I just mentioned, but it was not super great. To get the horse to back up with any kind of try, you had to shake the lead rope pretty hard, and sometimes once you

started to shake hard, instead of backing up faster the horse would come forward or go sideways. So we filmed us working on these things just to refine them a little bit more, and then everything started to look pretty good.

Next I said, "Okay, let's go set it up just how it always is with your husband leading his horse walking in front of you and your horse. Let's do it exactly how you guys have done it in the past." I was hoping the horse would still try to rush through the gate so my aunt could have the practice of being ready to send a big wave up the lead rope and get the horse to stop and stand before it had the idea to take off.

I explained to her that a lot of fixing this would be to get a feel for when the horse was thinking about bolting, get there beforehand, and have the horse do something else instead. I told her that she could simply stop the horse, or have it back up a few steps -- really just about anything to redirect its thought pattern, because if she didn't intervene, the path that the horse is thinking on its own would lead to bolting through the gate.

Aunt Jackie had the idea and was watching the horse carefully as she was walking towards the gate. Her husband had already gone through and I told her, "Okay, before you get to the gate, stop the horse and have it back up a few times, then walk a few more steps forward, and then stop and back the horse up again." She was about 20 feet from the gate and gradually walking and getting the horse closer and closer to the gate, but every few steps she would stop and get the horse to back up a few. After about 40 seconds, she was standing right in the middle of the gate and the horse was standing there not trying to go forward at all. Previously, this was where the horse would rush past her, so I reminded her to be ready. But the horse was doing very good staying 12 feet back away from her. I said, "Keep your feet planted and just pull on the lead and get the horse to take about three steps towards you and then shake the lead and stop the horse." That part went good, so I said, "Now back

the horse up one step and then bring it five steps closer to you. Good. Now, back it up a couple of steps and bring it three steps closer. Very good. Now just stop right there and see if the horse will stand, but be ready to really start shaking the lead if the horse even starts to take a single step forward."

We stood there for three minutes and the horse never took a single step. If it would have, she would have needed to catch that and put the horse back where she left it. But there was no need. After standing for a few minutes testing the horse, I told her to walk on through the gate. Now she was standing about 10 feet inside of the pasture. I instructed her to stop the horse when it got right to the middle of the gate. She did that nicely, the horse stopped, and there was no confusion on the horse's part.

I told her to walk a few more steps into the pasture, reel the horse in a few more steps, and then stop the horse and back him all the way back through the gate. For about two minutes, we practiced having the horse walk through the gate and about 10 feet into the pasture. Her job was to stand about 10 or 15 feet inside of the pasture and face the gate. The horse's job was to continue facing her and go forward and backwards, like reeling a yo-yo in and out, back and forth through gate. The whole time the horse was facing her. For the horse, it would be like seven steps forward, seven steps back, and then repeat.

After doing this several times, I instructed her to reel the horse all the way in to where she was standing (which was about 15 feet inside of the pasture) and then take off the halter and walk away. She did this and the horse stood right there the whole time, and then calmly walked off once she turned him loose.

The point of this story is that once we were able to get the horse to understand and think a little more about respecting personal space, and being nice and light on the end of a halter, by the time we actually got to the gate, the horse's mind was already different than it normally would have been. She asked me if it would be necessary to go through that lengthy of a process just to put the horse in the pasture, and I explained to her that it all depends; if the horse has been living the habit of bolting through the gate for the past five years, you may have to do it for a week or so to really get the horse certain that it is a different game now. But I said to her, "If you can be really consistent about this, in no time at all you will simply just lead the horse out and turn it into the pasture without having to do all of these extra steps." I told her to think of it as teaching a kid to read. In the beginning, you might have to give him a good bit of help and let him know when he was off a little bit, but after a while all you do is put the book in front of him and say, "Read this."

CHAPTER 43
IT'S NEVER THE HORSE'S FAULT

This has been mentioned earlier in the book, but I wanted to hit on it again because it's such an important concept. I interact with horse owners every day, and often hear people say things like, "That horse is disrespectful." Or, "He is just a pushy horse." Or, "Yes, he's pretty hot and always going really fast, but that's just him." Or, "This horse has got a bad attitude. He always tries to outthink the rider." It goes on and on and on, but you have to realize that none of those statements are an accurate assessment of the situation. If anything, those are subconscious ways to make an excuse for ourselves. It's very easy to say, "Well, instead of me trying to learn how to fix this, I'll just pawn it off and say, 'That is just the type of horse he is.'" But you see, if you are thinking like that, you will never improve and, more than likely, the horse won't either.

First, let's talk about the respect issue. Generally, people label a horse as disrespectful when he pushes into pressure or when he does something that the rider does not want. But you have to remember -- horses do not do things right and wrong. They do what they think is the easiest thing to do for the situation and the circumstances. If a horse is being pushy, it's not because he's trying to be disrespectful. It's because he does not have anything better to do. He does not know of anything better to do. If he did, he would simply do that instead.

A lot of people like to say, "This horse does not yield to pressure. He needs lessons on learning to yield to pressure." But yet, again, it goes back to the same old thing. You know how they say a horse is a flight or fight animal. First they try to flee, and if they cannot escape, they will then fight. In other words, if the horse is being pushy, it is because you are not doing a good enough job of giving him a way to escape that pressure, or at least good enough to where he realizes that there is an escape by doing _____. It could be any number of things, stopping, turning, side passing, et cetera.

Another thing about yielding to pressure --- if you have ever tried to put a halter on a wild horse or one with zero handling, you will notice that that horse is not pushy at all. A lot of times you end up spending at least the first three or four days just trying to get within five feet of the horse. Then somewhere along the way, over the course of the next 10 years, the horse ends up being a horse that runs people over. Was it that the horse was naturally respectful before the human got involved and once the human did get involved, they made him disrespectful by teaching him to crowd people?

Here's another one. You know how they say you should never trot a horse back to the barn. Well, if you can't trot your horse back to the barn without him ending up running off with you or something horrible happening, then it is not trotting back to the barn that caused the problem. Trotting back to the barn is just what made the problem show up.

I hear people say that their horse is stubborn and doesn't want to cooperate. But, that would be physically impossible if it is the horse's idea to do what you are asking. A horse cannot be stubborn about doing something that he actually wants to do. Everything with a horse, good and bad, is our fault.

Yes, a horse can learn to do what people call 'take advantage' of a human, but I've got another scenario here. Let's say that a horse rears up when you want it to back up. Well, a lot of people would say, "Boy, that horse has your number," or they may say something like, "Boy, that horse is really taking advantage of that person." Now, let's look at the exact opposite of that. Let's look at a horse that when you barely pick up the reins, he starts flying backwards super fast with a beautiful head position. He picks up his feet nicely and backs just as fast and as far as you would ever want him to, never having to use more than an ounce of

pressure. Everyone would look at that and say, "Boy, what a nice broke horse. That horse is so light." But, if you really think about it from the horse's perspective, the horse that backed up real nice did the same thing as the horse that reared up. Both horses in both scenarios figured out a way to avoid having pressure put on them. They both figured out how to take advantage of the rider. They both figured out how to do something to keep the rider from pulling on them. Think about that one for a couple of minutes.

As long as we're taking a break from the stories and discussing a little more about horses, I would like to also remind you just how much everything is interconnected. Here's an example: let's say that a horse becomes barn-sour. Well, if that horse is always ridden with a little bit of tension on the reins when he is out on the trail, in the arena, or wherever, and if he is always ridden in a saddle that does not fit him very well, and the cinch is always overly tightened making him extremely uncomfortable, and then the rider is always bouncing and swaying left and right all over the horse's back making him feel like he's going to lose his balance every step and then, all of a sudden, that horse gets back to the barn and it all goes away. Everything gets very pleasant again. This could very easily and very quickly make a horse barn-sour. It may not even take more than a few rides.

The reason it's important to be able to correctly ride a horse and not make him feel like he is about to lose his balance is because a horse is a flight animal. They rely on being able to move their feet to flee and escape danger. If your horse is feeling that he cannot easily move his body and his feet, then that can make a spooky horse.

Here's another one. Let's say the rider's technique of mounting their horse is really bad. Every time they get on the horse, whether from a mounting block or on the ground, they are pulling really hard out to the side. This is doing a couple of things. For one, it's making the horse feel like he's going to lose his balance. That can make a horse insecure about being mounted and being ridden. The second thing this could do is make the cinch pinch the skin underneath his belly. It could also make a saddle that fits decent become very uncomfortable because of all of the heavy sideways pulling. Bad mounting technique could also cause the cinch to have to be overly tightened, therefore making the saddle uncomfortable to the horse. If the mounting technique was good, and the rider could mount the horse without pulling the saddle off to the side, there would be no need to over tighten the cinch, and this would make the saddle much more comfortable for the horse. This alone can make a horse barn-sour. This alone can make a horse begin pinning his ears and turning around to nip at the rider when they're saddling or getting on. This alone can cause a horse to do all of the common horse problems that we hear about.

With a horse that is tagged as 'disrespectful' ---- the reason it is so important that the horse does not move YOUR feet is because, in horse world, that would be telling the horse that HE is the leader. If you are inconsistent, meaning some days you say, "Okay, I'm the leader," and other days you tell him he is the leader, he is going to see that inconsistency and that will come off to him as having uncertain leader. Therefore, he will have no choice but to ignore your request (be 'disrespectful'), and he will have to take his own reins and be the leader because you are not. It is critical that a horse has a leader. It is required. It's wired into their mentality. The inconsistency in the leadership of the human is why you see inconsistency in horses. It's all interconnected. Man, it felt good to get that off my chest. Not to make people feel bad, but to make them aware of these vital truths, and attempt to be an advocate for the horses of the world.

CHAPTER 44
WHAT'S NEXT?

After reading this book you may be a bit overwhelmed with the knowledge and strategies you've learned. And you're probably wondering where to start with your horse. I personally have a very structured system that I take my horses through. It starts with earning respect and then I begin desensitizing. After that we move on to the groundwork and then to the riding fundamentals. Once the horse understands the fundamentals, we progress through some intermediate riding and then move into advanced riding.

Here's the good news. I have 8 online video training courses that walk you through every step of the way. It's the exact system I use to take a horse from not knowing anything at all to doing advanced stuff like sliding stops, spins, rollbacks, etc. So it doesn't matter what level your horse is at. You can start at the beginning, in the middle, or wherever you need to get him to the level you want him.

And while going through the courses you'll encounter many videos from the stories you've read in this book. That's right, a large portion of these stories were written from videos in my courses.

You'll get access to all 8 of my courses when you sign up for the Carson James membership...

- Horsemanship
- Earning Respect
- Desensitizing
- Groundwork
- Riding Fundamentals
- Intermediate Riding
- Advanced Riding
- Problem Solving

Plus you'll get direct access to me through the members only online group. You can talk directly to me and ask me any questions you may encounter along your journey to better horsemanship. I'm always there to lend a helping hand.

You can sign up for a FREE 30-day trial to the Carson James Membership here: https://sp.carsonjames.com/trial (Please don't share this. You're getting this special link because you bought the book.)

I hope this book has given you some direction and aid for improving your horsemanship. I've tried my very best to share from the depths of my mind and explain things the best way I know how. I hope it helps create a better life for both you and your horse. And with that I will end this book. Thank you so much for reading, and I wish you all the success in the world.

Sincerely,

Carson James

ABOUT THE AUTHOR

Photo by Andi Harmon

Carson James takes horsemanship back to its original and pure form. His experience working for large ranches in the northwest, for performance trainers, and riding thousands of 'problem' horses around the country has given him the opportunity to practically apply the horsemanship skills he outlines in this book. His ability to break these concepts down into small and easily understandable steps sets him apart from many contemporary clinicians. He began his horsemanship journey as a teenager. He needed some cash in his pocket, so he started riding some local horses for folks just to keep them exercised. But he soon realized that his skills were lacking, and he was determined to find out what was really going on in the horse's mind. As his passion to become a skilled rider grew, he studied the great horsemen of the past, vaquero horsemanship, dressage, and anything else he could get his hands on. Then he worked for some performance trainers and surrounded himself with guys who were really handy horseback on some big ranches in the northwest. He rode horse after horse not only getting a job done but allowing each one to teach him something new. It was a lot of trial and error, but he found that no matter what level a horse is at, or what 'problems' he is having, every single horse will respond when you apply true horsemanship. Now he make hundreds of horse training videos for his membership site -- http://members.carsonjames.com -- and travels around the country conducting clinics to impart to others what the horses have taught him.

Made in the USA
Columbia, SC
16 January 2018